'One of the most common charges [...] initiatives in the church is that they d[...] delighted to see this honest and enco[...] work in Norfolk that has endured and in[...] thirty years. In this helpful account of faith, fellowship [...] see the faithfulness of God to those who seek to follow Him.'
Rev Canon J.John

'This is a highly instructive and inspiring story of rural renewal. But what makes it so much more valuable is that it recounts one of the most innovative adventures in rural mission. Stephen (and Martin before him) is one of the most releasing leaders we know and this is what has led to a lay movement of multiplying diverse expressions of Church across Norfolk. His exposition provides a picture of what a truly biblical "resourcing church" can look like in the twenty-first century.'
Rev Bob Hopkins and Mary Hopkins, ACPI and Fresh Expressions

'I am so pleased that Stephen Mawditt has written this book. Pippa and I are most grateful to him and Martin Down for all their visionary support over the years. Stephen is a pioneer of the faith whose passion for telling people the good news of Jesus has changed lives and been an inspiration to many, many people.'
Rev Nicky Gumbel, Holy Trinity Brompton

'So many of our stories of church and kingdom growth are set in cities, with their many advantages, obvious and less obvious. What a joy to read a tested and ongoing story of mission and service in a place that might never get the headlines but where God's heart for people and the power of His Spirit to transform have been proven to be just as great!'
Rev Paul Harcourt, national leader, New Wine England

'Stephen Mawditt has done a great service to the Church by writing down the story of Fountain of Life Church. He describes, in story after story, its journey from small beginnings to being a church that is resourcing the wider area, working with their bishop, planting congregations and missional communities, developing ministries that are touching the lives of so many people, and giving away all that God has grown within their midst. I loved the combination of the church being led by the Spirit of God, with leaders making courageous, faith-filled decisions, people coming to faith in Christ, the generosity of the people of God on a mission to love their neighbours and give to bless the wider Church, and a growing vision that has been worked out in practical, down-to-earth ways. It is an inspiring read and a great encouragement to the huge number of rural churches in England to identify and make space for other rural resource churches to bring growth and transformation afresh in their own areas. We need more Fountains of Life!'

Rt Rev Ric Thorpe, Bishop of Islington

'Testimonies of faith inspire us and remind us that we serve a God who loves to do extraordinary things through ordinary people. That is what *Redigging the Wells* does – it will inspire you and remind you of how Jesus transforms people's lives through His Church and the wonderful things that can come from a community of His people who are ready to step out in faith in response to His call.'

Rev John McGinley, director of Church Planting Development, New Wine England

'God did a new thing in rural Norfolk when the Fountain of Life was born. An experience of renewal; a longing to serve; a mission to evangelise; a commitment to a rural location; a willingness to take risks for Christ – these were all elements in this adventure of faith. So too were the challenges of creating a new congregation. There were growing pains. The story is not one without cost, but there is no authentic Christianity without suffering to overcome.

'The growth of the Fountain of Life has continued. The Holy Spirit has led the congregation and its leadership in directions they did not think they were called to go. There was a lot of faithful listening and discernment. It was this openness to God's future which meant it was a privilege for me to be the Bishop of Norwich for most of the first two decades of the Fountain of Life's existence. God blessed this adventure of faith. His blessings continue. There is much to learn from Stephen Mawditt's excellent account. May the Fountain of Life long continue to be the bearer of streams of living water in God's Church.'

Rt Rev Graham James, Bishop of Norwich 1999–2019

Redigging the Wells

A REMARKABLE ACCOUNT
OF RURAL RENEWAL

Stephen Mawditt

instant
ap◻stle

First published in Great Britain in 2021

Instant Apostle
104 The Drive
Rickmansworth
Herts
WD3 4DU

Author's agent: The Tony Collins Literary Agency.

British Library Cataloguing-in-Publication Data

A catalogue record for this book is available from the British Library.

This book and all other Instant Apostle books are available from Instant Apostle:

Website: www.instantapostle.com

Email: info@instantapostle.com

ISBN 978-1-912726-49-3

Printed in Great Britain.

For Pippa – my beloved wife, best friend and faithful companion on the journey

Contents

Acknowledgements

My thanks to the Fountain of Life Church. You are an inspiration, and Pippa and I have loved being your leaders. Some of you are named in this book, others are not, but all of you have played a part in the story recorded here. Know that we carry you all close to our hearts. A simple thank you seems insufficient. We love you.

Thank you to Pippa for being my co-leader, allowing me to have the space and time to write this book, and without whom the journey would have been shorter and considerably less fun. Thank you, too, to Simon. Life in the vicarage must have been challenging at times but I am so proud to call you my son.

Thank you to Martin who went before me and pioneered a way. Thank you also to Bishop Graham James who made space for me to flourish and who shared the journey with us. Thank you to our friends at New Wine and Holy Trinity Brompton for their encouragement and inspiration. A special thanks to Bob and Mary Hopkins, who have been our faithful accompaniers on the journey. Anything that is good in this book probably came from one of you!

Thank you to all those who have led alongside me in a paid or unpaid capacity. It is your commitment, sacrifice and gifting that has enabled us to punch above our weight and see the kingdom come.

Thank you to the many quoted people who gave permission for their stories to be told, and to Maureen Payne for proofreading the accuracy of my words. I have done my best to present the story accurately but of course all errors are mine.

Thank you to Instant Apostle for adopting me into your family, especially to Nicki for her faith in the book, Sheila for her editing skills in significantly improving it and to Anne and Nigel for their creativity in design and presentation – and to Tony Collins for making the introduction.

Finally, and above all, this is the story of Jesus building His Church. Thank You, Jesus, for calling me, equipping me and being faithful to me. I have attempted to write for Your glory for Your endorsement is all I seek.

Foreword
Rev Martin Down

'I was young and now I am old' (Psalm 37:25), and I tell you that nothing in life is so exciting and rewarding as seeing God changing lives as people come into His kingdom. This book is the story of a place where God has been doing this for more than thirty years and is doing it still. It is a very ordinary place, a village in Norfolk, and a story of very ordinary people – except that God can take very ordinary people and make them extraordinary.

I am the leader of the church in this place when the story begins, and Stephen has been the leader of that same church up to where the story ends – for now. God is the same from beginning to end.

I hope that this book will inspire other churches, other leaders and other members of the body of Christ in many different places to believe that God can do for them and in their place what He has done for us and for this church in Norfolk. I hope in particular that other churches will learn from our accumulated experience, and will be inspired to imitate, not the things that we have done, but the values and principles on which we have done them: values and principles that Stephen sums up at the end of the book.

On a personal note, I want to pay tribute to Stephen, with whom I worked side by side for twelve years. No church leader could have had a more faithful and loyal colleague, and I rejoice beyond words at how God has blessed the church and Stephen's ministry since then. Next, I want to express my love and admiration for all the dear people about whom you will read in this book. Some were there at the very beginning, of whom some are still there, and some have gone to be with the Lord. Others have come to the Lord and joined the church over the intervening years; I love you all. It is these men and women, their devotion, their gifts and their faithfulness, that have built this church and extended the kingdom of God in this place.

One other person I want to mention is one whose name appears once or twice in passing in this story: Graham James, who was the Bishop of Norwich from 1999 to 2019. His support and encouragement behind the scenes throughout these years was an untold blessing that underlies so much of what you will read here. But above all, of course:

To God be the glory.

Author's Preface

I am a reluctant author, having successfully resisted for several years the calls to set our story down. A reluctance perhaps spurred either by the sense most of us have that our story does not really matter, or by an unspoken fear that our story does not carry the weight or significance that we ourselves attach to it – or even that we shall do a disservice to the story by attempting to put it into words.

Perhaps I am cautious that in telling our story, I may encourage ourselves, or others, to seek to reproduce it in a way that causes us to miss what God uniquely wants to do in and through us, today, to reach our communities with the good news of the gospel of Jesus Christ. Or, even worse, that in a perverse way, hearing our story might cause others to be discouraged or devalue the work God has done in their own situations or contexts.

Perhaps, though, my reluctance is born out of my own insecurities that in telling the story, some may be critical of the decisions I have overseen and my shortcomings as a leader will be exposed. But any reluctance I have felt is now overshadowed by the compulsion of the Holy Spirit to write 'an account of the things that have been fulfilled among us' (Luke 1:1), and that is proving stronger than any human voice, and ultimately irresistible!

So I hope and pray that what is to come proves to be a source of strength, encouragement and empowerment to all those involved in leading within God's kingdom – especially perhaps those who, like me, respond to God's call with something like, 'Surely, Lord, there must be someone more qualified than I to do this,' or who identify with one or other of the perfectly understandable excuses given by Moses, culminating in, 'Please send someone else' (Exodus 4:13)!

This is the story of one particular church in the Church of England, the Fountain of Life. Initially formed as a missionary congregation in the summer of 1996, under the apostolic leadership of Martin Down, we have grown to become a network and resource church within the diocese of Norwich.

Our story begins eight years earlier in December 1988, when Martin was appointed to lead two parish churches, St Nicholas' and St George's, set in the villages of Ashill and Saham Toney respectively, each with a population of around 1,600 at that time. It was out of these two churches that the Fountain of Life was formed. Pippa and I join the story in 1993 when, attracted by Martin's vision, we moved to serve these two churches initially in a lay capacity before I was ordained as an Anglican priest in 1996, the same year as the Fountain of Life was formed.

Martin led the Fountain of Life from its formation in 1996 to early 2005 and I, having served as his curate during that time, succeeded him as senior leader until the summer of 2019 when my associate, Paul Wilkinson, in turn succeeded me. It's a story that has continued through the planned succession of senior leadership on two occasions, which is highly unusual within our denomination. This continuity of leadership is reflected in both Martin's foreword and the text of an interview I conducted with Paul in February 2021 which is included as Appendix Four. In this interview I also explore with Paul something of the impact of Covid-19 upon the life of the church, as the main story told in this book finishes in 2019. Despite the current challenges brought about by the pandemic, the church has successfully transitioned through two leadership successions and now enters into the blessings of third-generational leadership – and I now apparently have time to write this book!

Our story is set within the context of rural Britain, deep in the heart of Norfolk, a county renowned for its open skies, coastlines, the Broads and a diocese with more than 650 largely medieval churches. So it's a story that will perhaps especially connect with those involved in rural ministry. As a network church, we do not work within the usual parochial boundaries of the Church of England – our limits are set by those we are in relationship with and are seeking to reach with the good news of the gospel. Borrowing words from John Wesley, we 'look upon all the world as [our] parish'.[1] Ours is a story that resonates with how God has been moving by His Spirit across our nation in churches of all shapes and sizes, streams and denominations, colours and forms. As a church, we are inevitably shaped by our Anglican roots, but more so by the values and vision of desiring to see the kingdom of God come, lives transformed by knowing Jesus and our communities enriched and infused with life in the Spirit.

It's a story set within a changing Church landscape, especially within the Church of England over the past three decades, and as such is a commentary on those times. When we first set out, church planting was anathema within the Church of England; parish boundaries were sacred; there was no vocabulary to describe what we were doing, and there were very few models of new forms of church, especially in a rural setting. We were pioneering, resisting the pressure of an institution to conform to itself, making bold statements, probably seen at times as the angry, discontented teenager rebelling against authority, and sometimes acting as one! We were a small group of people, initially a raft of a few more than twelve committed families, who set out on a journey to engage in mission. It was at times turbulent and uncertain but always blessed by God and huge fun.

Press the 'fast forward' button and it is as if we live in a different world. The *Mission-Shaped Church* report in 2004[2] gave

---

[1] Dr Blake, 'The World is my Parish or My Parish is the world', Wesley's Horse, 29th October 2017, wesleyshorse.com/the-world-is-my-parish-or-my-parish-is-the-world (accessed 13th May 2021).
[2] *Mission-Shaped Church* (London: Church House Publishing, 2004).

a vocabulary and validation to the work we were doing. Then along came Fresh Expressions of Church, the language of 'mixed economy'[3] under Rowan Williams as Archbishop of Canterbury, a national church-planting programme pioneered by Nicky Gumbel and Holy Trinity Brompton,[4] New Wine's commitment to equip and support church planters,[5] streams of lay and ordained pioneer ministry within the Church of England and strategic development funding released to dioceses by the new Archbishop of Canterbury, Justin Welby. Suddenly parish boundaries are porous, all things are possible and, within the institution of the Church of England, we have moved from being a provocative voice on the margins to being recognised as a resource church at the centre of diocesan plans. By 2019, our church membership had grown to more than 300, and we were in a discipling relationship with at least a further 300 through our missional communities, the concept of which is explored in Chapter 7.

Wherever possible I shall tell the story grammatically in the first person plural because it is the story of community, of team, of a group of people who have persistently and consistently sought to partner with God in the extraordinary adventure and crazy notion of seeing the kingdom come through the Church.[6] This is our story.

It's a story of the power of the Holy Spirit at work to bring renewal and transformation to individuals, congregations and

[3] The term was introduced by Archbishop Rowan Williams to enable fresh expressions and 'inherited' forms of church to be equally valued, respected and supported within the same denomination, see freshexpressions.org.uk/find-out-more/going-deep-1-the-mixed-economy/ (accessed 13th April 2021).

[4] www.htb.org/ (accessed 25th January 2021).

[5] New Wine's vision is to see local churches changing nations. See www.new-wine.org/ (accessed 25th January 2021).

[6] Greek *basileia*, translated as 'kingdom', interpreted as meaning the rule or reign of God. In Matthew 16:18-19 Jesus promises to build the Church and give (to us) 'the keys of the kingdom'.

structures. A story of a group of people choosing to be family together, willing to step out onto the waters, take risks and have an adventure of a lifetime following Jesus. It's our story, but above all it is God's story, and because of that it's a story of hope.

It has already been partially recorded by the founder of the Fountain of Life, Martin Down, in books that are now out of print.[7] I have drawn from material in these books to recount the early years leading up to the planting of the Fountain of Life.

Ours is an unfinished story. A story of journey, not arrival. It chronicles events before Covid-19 and it feels as if our story has to almost begin again. We have to find ourselves afresh in this new landscape. It's no good us returning to where we have come from. It's a new day. There's a new vista. There are new stories to learn from. Yet, history is important. It reminds us of the faithfulness of God, that He never gives up on us, that He is always for us – making a way against all the odds. We need to recapture the romance of the adventure. Church is family, it's supposed to be fun and there is such immense freedom intended for the leader who follows in the footsteps of the 'pioneer and perfecter' of our faith (Hebrews 12:2).

This is our story. Your story will be different. This is not a model to be transferred, nor do we have all the answers. Above all, I hope that our story of God doing an extraordinary work through ordinary people in the unlikeliest of locations will bring glory to God and inspire you afresh to know that, however challenging your situation, nothing is impossible for the God who is with you and 'is able to do immeasurably more than all we ask or imagine' (Ephesians 3:20).

I should like to thank all those whose names appear in this book for their permission to include something of their story

---

[7] Martin Down, *Speak to These Bones* (Tunbridge Wells: Monarch Publications, 1993); Martin Down, *Streams of Living Water* (Crowborough: Monarch Publications, 1996); Martin Down, *Building a New Church Alongside the Old* (Eastbourne: Kingsway, 2003).

and all those who, though not named here, have also been part of our journey. We could not have travelled so far without you.

Oh, and one more thing before we begin. It comes from a dear friend of mine, a member of our church, who recently said, 'Don't forget to tell them we had fun.'

Introduction

'So, what's your vision?' was Maureen's opening question as she welcomed my wife, Pippa, and I into her home for the first time and hung our coats in the hallway. One day, towards the end of 1992, her husband, Martin, had phoned and invited us over for a meal. So, here we were, looking forward to a convivial evening and expecting the usual courtesies or pleasantries of 'How are you?', 'How was your journey?', 'How lovely to see you!' or, 'Can I get you a drink?' Maureen's question was rather more challenging and required a longer answer.

It transpired that when Maureen had asked Martin, 'Why are these people coming for a meal?' his reply had been, 'Well, I've no idea but I sensed the Holy Spirit wanting me to invite them over.' Understandably, Maureen was intrigued to find out more.

Before we answer Maureen's question, let's introduce ourselves – first Martin and Maureen, then ourselves.

As a child, Martin had attended church and Sunday school but, during his teenage years, he had resisted a clear sense of the Lord's calling on his life, and gradually his faith faded. By the time he entered the University of Cambridge, he was describing himself as an agnostic. But in Martin's second year at university, God spoke to him one morning during November 1960.

We had a short conversation in my room: he had not appeared, but his words had been audible to me and I had been shaken to the very core. It was a week before I could continue any academic work at all and two years before I was able to say the simple yes that he required of me. But as I walked home through the wood behind our house one September evening two years later, I surrendered my life to Jesus, as my Lord and my long-suffering Saviour.[8]

Three years later, Martin entered the ministry of the Church of England knowing that he was called to be a missionary sent to preach the gospel and win men and women for Christ, and 'with a love for the English countryside, village life and country parishes'.[9] In the early 1970s, Martin heard about the charismatic movement and attended a conference led by Michael Harper of the Fountain Trust on the 'baptism of the Holy Spirit'.[10] Ten years later, having been challenged by the experience of a friend and church member who had experienced being filled with the Holy Spirit, Martin found himself attending a Full Gospel Businessmen's[11] dinner and listening to Bishop Richard Hare. His words resonated with Martin's experience and so at the end he asked a friend who had accompanied him to ask God to fill him with His Holy Spirit. Martin comments:

> It was not a sensational experience. I was not 'slain' by the Spirit[12] and I did not feel light or warmth. In fact I did not feel anything. Immediately afterwards I wondered if anything had happened at all. But as the days and weeks and months followed I knew that that evening had worked a greater change in me than any since the one

---

[8] Down, *Speak to These Bones*, p18.

[9] Ibid, p19.

[10] This is a term interpreted in a variety of ways by different denominations, streams and traditions. Baptism of (with or in) the Spirit in our theological understanding is an immersion into the empowering presence of God.

[11] www.fgbuk.org/ (accessed 16th March 2021).

[12] The term 'slain in (by) the Spirit' is a term used in charismatic and Pentecostal circles to describe the physical reaction of a person falling to the ground when being filled with the Holy Spirit and encountering the presence of God. See for example Acts 9:3-4; Revelation 1:17.

when I had first surrendered my life to God in 1962. It was 29th June 1983.[13]

The change may not have been immediately apparent to Martin, but it was to others. One parishioner at the time was heard to say to another, 'What's happened to the vicar? He's gone all religious!'

Maureen too had a Christian upbringing, had attended Church of England schools and been confirmed, but after leaving school had lost her links to church and Christianity. Several years later she had returned to church, influenced by the example of her previous head teacher and her boss, who she knew were both Christians. She 'learned the truth about God and about the sacrifice of Christ ... and learnt that a personal commitment to Christ was necessary'.[14] One day while walking in Hyde Park, Maureen too made her commitment to Him. Soon after this, she met Martin and found herself married to an Anglican curate. She became immersed in the business of 'making homes, raising children and being the vicar's wife'.[15] In terms of her relationship with God, though, there was a sense of remoteness and distance about her Christian experience. It all seemed unreal.

So she came to be sitting alongside her husband listening to Richard Hare speaking about his experience. Like Martin, she was open to anything that God might want to give her and she too went forward to be prayed with to be filled with the Holy Spirit:

> Nothing dramatic happened at the time, but soon afterwards other people began to notice the difference in her; even her daughter, then aged fifteen, remarked that Mum was happier. Indeed, Maureen, without being fully aware of it, had never been truly happy for as long as she

[13] Down, *Speak to These Bones*, p22.
[14] Down, *Building a New Church Alongside the Old*, pp20-21.
[15] Ibid, p21.

could remember, but now she found springing up inside her a little fountain of joy which had never been there before and which, despite many hardships and difficulties, has never gone away.[16]

Now, after a break in ministry outside the Church of England, Martin and Maureen returned to parish ministry, taking up their new roles in the heart of Norfolk in 1988.

Pippa and I also moved to Norfolk in 1988. We had both come to faith at Holy Trinity Brompton (HTB) – Pippa in 1980 and me a year later. As a child, Pippa went to church with her family and, during her time at boarding school from the age of ten, experienced chapel daily. On leaving school, she moved away from home to train as a nurse and went less often to church. There were times when she tried to pray but didn't feel that there was anyone to hear her. Some years later, a friend suggested that she accompany her to church at HTB. She found it welcoming, lively and modern, made friends with a nurse from the same hospital and joined an Enquirers group to find out more. After a while she felt that she should take a decision to follow Jesus but was hesitant as she felt that she was taking a step into the dark. God spoke to her through Revelation 3:20: 'Here I am! I stand at the door and knock. If anyone hears my voice and opens the door, I will come in and eat with that person, and they with me.' She knew that Jesus was knocking at the door of her heart and all she had to do was open the door and invite Him in. So she did. She felt a great sense of relief and peace, was able to trust God and knew He was with her.

I had less of a Christian upbringing. We were not a churchgoing family and I did not attend Sunday school. It wasn't that I didn't believe in God, but I certainly had no comprehension about Jesus or interest in finding out anything more. As far as I knew, none of my friends were Christians and I was not aware of a particular gap or need in my life. I

16 Ibid, pp21-22.

remember praying at times – especially as a child – and every time I prayed it did feel as if things turned out better than I had expected.

Then God positioned someone into my life. He was an American, of similar age to myself, who came to work for six months in my department. One day he asked me if I was a Christian and, although I answered positively, we both suspected that the real answer was 'no'. Our friendship developed and I found myself attending church with him, going to the same Enquirers group that Pippa had attended. I came to realise that the life and resurrection of Jesus as portrayed in the Gospels was true and required a response. I struggled with the idea of my commitment to Him until it was pointed out to me that on the cross Jesus demonstrated His total commitment to me. All I needed to do was accept that, respond to it, welcome Him into my life and surrender control to Him. He would do the rest. So as best I could, I did.

We both separately went on the Alpha course at HTB,[17] which at that time was intended for those who had already taken the decision to follow Jesus. This was before Nicky Gumbel restructured the course, recognising its evangelistic potential, which has released Alpha to be the global phenomenon that it is. I then joined a home group and found myself listening to an attractive young lady giving a rather strange story. She had been to a seminar on living in the fullness of the Holy Spirit. As she was prayed for she 'experienced an overwhelming sense of God's love – when I was in bed that night I received the gift of tongues[18] and couldn't go to sleep because I was praising the Lord'. I was not at all sure what that was all about at the time,

---

[17] Alpha is the best course I know for exploring the foundations of the Christian faith. Over eleven weeks it is a safe place to gather those who do not yet know Jesus for a conversation about faith. See www.alpha.org (accessed 25th January 2021).

[18] The gift of a prayer language referred to in the book of Acts and described more fully in 1 Corinthians 12-14. I shall refer to this gift in more detail in Chapter 10.

but it was my first encounter with Pippa. We would go on to lead a home group, attend various training courses, serve on mission teams – and our friendship blossomed into love and marriage in September 1984. I often say that we ended up attending so many different events and activities together that it just made economic sense for us to get married and share the cost of fuel! Our son, Simon, was born the following year. At this time, we lived in Clapham and I managed a company based in London while Pippa was a nurse until Simon was born (although, rather like vicars, nurses never 'retire'!).

Following coming to faith, we had always considered that our livelihood would be directly connected to overtly Christian activities, and after three years of marriage we sensed the Holy Spirit was on our case saying that the time was now. We asked a few people to pray for us and there were various 'words' and 'pictures' that seemed to be confirming 'this was the time'.[19] Someone had a picture of an A–Z road map of London with our road highlighted, and the highlight continued off the page. The image had our road positioned exactly as on the map. Someone else had the promise from Isaiah 40:11 'that God would lead those who have young gently',[20] a great encouragement for a couple with a two-year-old. So, we started praying and talking together about what the Lord might be calling us to step into. Two options that often seemed to surface were either that I should explore ordination within the Church of England or we should both be involved in running a Christian conference centre. At the time, ordination was not at all on my radar and we had benefited so much from weekends away at the latter. So we pursued the second option. The very first appointment that we applied for was at Letton Hall, a Christian conference and residential centre based in the deepest

---

[19] The language of 'words' and 'pictures' is used in this context to describe the way in which we hear from God for ourselves or other people. It can be a thought, an image or an impression given by the Holy Spirit to reveal truth about a situation or person.
[20] Paraphrase.

heart of rural Norfolk. Six months later we were appointed as wardens to start at Easter in 1988. We imagined that our time in Norfolk would be relatively brief. God had other ideas.

Moving from life in the metropolis to the remoteness of Letton was challenging – especially for Pippa, moving away from a close-knit church community and with a young child. It took a while for it to feel like home and probably, in truth, it never did. Our time at Letton was challenging in many ways, but it proved to be the place in which a vision and heart was formed in us to see renewal and revival come to Norfolk. Having lived in London, we were immediately very aware of how 'forgotten' anywhere east of the A1 seemed to be at that time and sensed that there was a movement of God stirring. The trustees of Letton Hall sensed our wider calling too and so, a little shy of three years, our season there finished at the end of 1990.

When we moved to Letton, we bought a cottage nearby and so we retreated there to take stock and work out what the Spirit might be saying next. I became aware of the difficulties facing those experiencing unemployment or redundancy and, as my previous work experience had been within the career counselling industry, I starting a Christian charity called Action Workwise. We provided services both to employers effecting redundancies and to individuals directly. One of our activities was to establish contact points in villages to make advice and practical help on job searching more freely available.

Martin and the Parochial Church Council (PCC)[21] at St Nicholas' were aware of the increase of people in their community who were facing hardship as a result of experiencing sudden and unexpected loss of employment and livelihood. I had written to local church leaders inviting them to contact us if they would like to establish a contact point in their village. My letter arrived in his morning post at just the right time and we were invited to establish a contact point in the village at the local Call-In – a local community gathering point – which was a great

---

[21] The PCC is the legal form of governance in a parish church.

place to meet because it was known in the village and accessible to all. We supported a number of individuals who came, some of whom were connected to the parish churches and others who were not.[22] More importantly in the context of our story, it was Action Workwise that forged the connection with Martin and Maureen.

So, here we were, towards the end of 1992, seated around Martin and Maureen's dining table talking about our heart and vision, and we discovered a real synergy between the four of us. By this time Martin had been rector at St Nicholas', Ashill, and St George's, Saham Toney, for four years. Over the course of the evening, Martin mentioned that members of St George's church were praying for a lay couple to move into the village who would exercise leadership in the church. At the time, I didn't particularly think any more about it, but on our way home the rather more prophetic Pippa said, 'Do you think the Lord might be calling us to do that?' So we talked and prayed about it, and I wrote Martin and Maureen a thank-you note for the meal including ten reasons as to why we thought that the Lord might be calling us!

I like to think there was another guest at that meal table, unseen but real enough, for Jesus always takes a keen interest in the conversations of His children, especially when it concerns His beloved bride, the Church (Malachi 3:16). I imagine He was chuckling to Himself as He listened to our thoughts and ideas, knowing how much more He was planning to do.

I expected the phone to ring immediately with a response, and was beginning to imagine that we had totally misread the situation. However, it transpired that Martin was already talking to people behind the scene, clearing the path for us to be interviewed by St George's PCC to assess whether or not we

---

[22] One of these was a lady called Derry. We helped her into employment. Twenty years later, our paths would cross again and a few years ago Derry completed the Alpha course with us, gave her life to Christ and joined the church. A great encouragement to value social action as indispensable to the work of mission and evangelism.

were the answer to their prayers. Soon we attended one of their meetings to be interviewed. A 'grilling' is a more accurate description. It was rather the sort of interview I would expect if we were going to be appointed as the incumbent. We had said to ourselves that we would only move if the PCC were unanimous, and they were. Somewhat miraculously, three months later we moved into the village of Saham Toney. Our position in the church was initially unpaid and undefined, but we knew we were called particularly to be alongside Martin and Maureen, and that was all we needed to know. I think our relationship was special to all of us as we journeyed together through what would prove to be such a formative period in the life of the churches.

So, let's set out on the journey that is this book. It's a story of redigging the wells of renewal and revival in rural England. We shall begin by recounting the early days, giving a taste of events that led to the emergence of 'The New Thing' that would become known as 'The Fountain of Life'. The first two chapters trace the story from Martin's arrival in 1988 through to my succession in 2005. These formative years laid the foundations for our future growth. In subsequent chapters, I have chosen to look at our growth and life together through the lens of nine key themes. As each chapter examines our whole story through a particular thematic lens, it can feel as if each chapter takes us back to the beginning of 'Day One', but it is the most effective way of telling the story.

Along the way, I shall attempt to point to some of the things we have learned, particularly so in my Final Word, where I shall summarise ten cultures of the church which have been helpful to keep in view.

Perhaps most important of all, this is a journey and story laced with tales of real people whose lives, like our own, have been touched and, in many cases, transformed by the love of God as they have come to know the person of Jesus Christ and the empowerment of the Spirit.

1
The New Thing

See, I am doing a new thing!
Now it springs up; do you not perceive it?
(Isaiah 43:19)

It all began in 1989 in the local village shop. Christine was married to John, one of the churchwardens at St Nicholas' Church, and with her husband ran an electrical retailer based in the village of Ashill. One evening, John and Christine had a meal with the new rector and his wife. During this, Christine mentioned that she had an appointment to see a medical consultant which she was rather apprehensive about.

The following day, Martin and Maureen visited Christine at work in her shop to find out what was wrong and to offer to pray for her. Christine told them that she had a much-enlarged ovary with a lump the size of an egg which she could feel in her stomach. Her doctor was concerned too and had referred her to a consultant who in turn had booked her in to have a scan. Much to Christine's surprise, Martin and Maureen prayed for her there and then. They laid hands on her and asked Jesus 'to make it so that when she goes to hospital the ovary is completely normal'.[23] That's exactly what happened.

---

[23] Down, *Speak to These Bones*, p27.

That's a wonderful thing. I got to the hospital and I had the scan. And the woman said, 'What are you here for? There is nothing wrong with you. Your ovaries are completely normal.' So, I'm perfectly alright. Isn't that amazing?[24]

Indeed it was, and Christine is still full of vigour and worshipping with us today. She describes her joy and love for Jesus as still growing, and has never forgotten what God did for her that day within the confines of her shop.

Martin came to these parishes with a loyalty to the Church of England and a heart to see the ancient churches 'full to overflowing with praising people and God moving in power in every place'.[25] Statistically the church was in decline, but God could change all that. The prophet Ezekiel had a vision of a valley full of dry bones (Ezekiel 37:1-14). It seemed impossible for them to live. But in his vision he was instructed to prophesy over them and command life. As he did, the bones were clothed in flesh, tendons formed and finally breath entered into the bones and they stood up – 'a vast army' (v10). This was God's word to Martin: 'Speak to these bones.' So he did.

From the outset Martin had invited response to the sermons he preached on Sundays, calling people forward for specific purposes. These included opportunities to commit or recommit their lives to Jesus, be filled with the Spirit, deal with specific issues of repentance or receive healing. His very first sermon concluded with an invitation to:

> Come and stand with me at the front of the church as a sign that you repent of your sins, that you want to claim the forgiveness which Jesus offers and that you commit your life with me to his obedience. This is not a ceremony. This is for real. Don't do it unless you mean

---

[24] Ibid, p28.
[25] Ibid, p14.

it. But if God is touching your heart to do this with me, come forward now.[26]

In one of the two churches, most came forward. Some were deeply moved by the experience. Sandra said, 'I had never done anything like that before in all the years I have been going to church. And ever since, I've felt great.'[27]

During his first Lent season in 1989, Martin held a midweek course to 'teach more about the person and work of the Holy Spirit to those who wanted to hear, and we began to put into practice what we learned: the ministry of healing, the exercise of the gifts of the Spirit, including the gift of tongues'.[28] Martin also began to take a small group of people to a summer conference called New Wine.[29]

As time went on, people who had been renewed in the power of the Holy Spirit grew in their desire for all that they were experiencing to be part of the regular Sunday experience in church. Space was given on a Sunday for prayer ministry. Testimonies began to abound. Someone who had suffered permanent damage to cartilage from playing football was greatly improved after prayer. Christine's daughter Louise came to visit. She was expecting a baby and experiencing some difficulties:

> She was suffering a good deal of pain and feeling quite ill six months into her pregnancy. She laid hands on her own stomach as we prayed over her. From that day on she felt fine and carried the baby for the rest of the time without trouble.[30]

---

[26] Ibid, p32.
[27] Ibid, p33.
[28] Down, *Building a New Church Alongside the Old*, p30.
[29] New Wine was formed in 1989 by Bishop David Pytches as an annual summer camp to encourage spiritual renewal and church growth across the country. See earlier note on p18.
[30] Down, *Speak to these Bones*, p67.

One Sunday morning, a year or two later, her husband, Adrian, surrendered his life to God and is now rector of four churches in Northamptonshire.

People were coming to faith and being baptised by immersion[31] – initially at the school's swimming pool, then at a local hotel. In those days no one would have anticipated that eventually most baptisms would take place in the comfort of our own heated, portable baptism pool.

It was an exciting time of growth in the life of the church, but not everyone was moving at the same speed. It was all too much, too soon for some. Not everyone appreciated the changes that were being introduced to worship and services. One lay minister resigned and joined another local church. There were difficulties to be overcome. These apply to any church welcoming spiritual renewal. There were issues of language, music, the place of children and young people, worship style and expression. Again, in Martin's words:

> There was trouble about the guitars and drums, about the new worship songs and the way we sang them, about dancing in church and about banners, about the public use of the gift of tongues, about words of knowledge, about the invocation of the Holy Spirit, about people laughing, crying and falling under the power of the Holy Spirit. We also stumbled over other issues which had been lying dormant in the church, including yoga, Freemasonry and extramarital partnerships.[32]

In these early years Martin was signposting the direction in which the church was heading and there would be no turning

---

[31] Baptism derives from the Greek word *baptizo* which means to plunge or immerse (Mark 1:9-10; Acts 8:36). When we lower a person into the water and raise them back up again, we graphically illustrate the way in which, when a person comes to faith, they have been cleansed from sin and raised to new life in Christ (Romans 6:3-4).

[32] Down, *Building a New Church Alongside the Old*, pp30-31.

back. Spiritual renewal challenges our values. It moves us from 'maintenance' mode to 'mission' mode, from 'church' to 'kingdom'. Our priorities change from being defined by the needs of the church to the needs of the world and the proclamation of the gospel.

With this in mind, in early 1993, Margaret, a member of the congregation, came to see Martin, having seen an article advertising an Alpha conference being held at HTB in the summer and she enthusiastically encouraged Martin to attend. He was keen to do so but would be on holiday at that time. So, knowing that Alpha had played a significant part in our story, Martin asked Pippa and me to attend on his behalf.

Since we had attended Alpha in the 1980s, HTB, through Nicky Gumbel, had seen the potential for it to be developed as an evangelistic tool. It was proving highly effective as a 'Come and See' invitation. The average number attending Alpha had significantly increased to an average of 500 per course and, with Alpha hosted termly, there were three courses each year. People were travelling to attend an Alpha course at HTB from as far afield as Salisbury and York. HTB wanted to equip local churches and leaders to run the course in their area. So, in June 1993 we headed down to London for this two-day training conference. We returned greatly enthused and very excited by the potential and vision behind Alpha, and eager to run our own courses.

We suggested initially encouraging both church congregations to attend. Alpha is a course that lays such a good foundation on what it means to be a Christian and how to live as a disciple that we felt it would be a helpful way of getting more people on to the same page in terms of vision and values. In particular, the focus on the person and work of the Holy Spirit would give a shared language and experience across the two churches. We also wanted to encourage people to come so that they would then invite others – experiencing Alpha for themselves would give people confidence to invite their not-yet-Christian family, friends and neighbours to come along too. So

34

we shared the vision with the two churches and recruited a team, including Margaret, who had first suggested Alpha, and her husband, Peter. We gathered the team together to prepare for the first Alpha course three days after moving into our new home in Saham Toney. We were surrounded by packing cases and somehow crammed everyone in, but we all left that first training evening sensing that God was beginning a new phase on our journey.

We ran the first Alpha course in September 1993. The take-up from both churches was encouraging – in the first year alone we ran three courses, each one attended by between fifty and seventy people. We met in one of the local schools. We started the first evening with a meal, then a talk on the topic of the evening, before breaking for refreshments and small group time. Martin and I shared the teaching and we made sure that we included the weekend on the theme of the Holy Spirit – although in our case this was squeezed into a Saturday's teaching. It is more difficult to encourage people already living in the countryside to see the value of a weekend away! This was so often the point in the course when people began to experience the love and power of God. It didn't always lead to conversion, though. I remember one person who was shaking on the spot describing the experience as feeling as if they were being electrocuted, but they still managed to walk away without making a commitment to following Jesus. However, many did make fresh or new commitments to following Him. It was an exciting time of growth in the church.

One person described themselves to me as being like a tall building. They said that before Alpha began, all was dark. But, week by week, a new floor was illuminated until by the end of the course the person felt as if the whole building was lit and they had moved from darkness to light.

There is no doubt that running Alpha accelerated the pace of renewal being experienced in both churches. Most commented that the opportunity to be filled with the Spirit had deepened their faith. Many had never heard the theology of the

Holy Spirit articulated so clearly. One seventy-eight-year-old lady wrote in the frontispiece of her Bible, 'Have been to church all my life and have finally discovered what it is all about.' Poignant and deeply moving.

Meanwhile, I needed a form of ministry that was authorised within the diocese, and it was agreed that it would be best for me to apply to be appointed as a reader.[33] This was approved and, as I was already some way through completing a diploma in theology, my diocesan training was shortened to one year. However, at the same time the diocese had decided to set up a new Ordained Local Ministry training course[34] and, with the encouragement and support of Martin and both PCCs, I applied. 1 had explored ordination upon leaving Letton Hall but the answer then had been 'no'. Although it is always easier to receive positive news, at the time I was content to accept the decision as I had applied more through the advice of others than sensing a firm conviction for myself. This time, though, I was sure that I was being called – I fully expected the answer to be positive, and it was.

So, three months after being licensed as a reader I set out on ordination training, to the chagrin of my reader tutor, who had been very impressed with an essay I wrote on the merits and need for effective lay leadership in churches. This is something I am still passionate about, but there is a place for ordained ministry too, and in due time I wanted to be in a position to lead a church within the Church of England if God so called.

Back home in the two parish churches, Martin further strengthened his leadership team. Alan was head teacher at a local school and had lived in the village for more than twenty years. Along with his wife, Susan, Alan had been one of the first to respond to the invitation to come forward to be baptised in the Spirit. He was ordained as a non-stipendiary minister in

---

[33] A form of authorised lay leadership within the Church of England.
[34] An alternative form of training ordained clergy to serve in the context of the local parish church, initially known as Local Non-Stipendiary Ministry.

1994. In the same year I was licensed as a reader and two years later I, too, was ordained. As a team, we shared in the public ministry of the church, leading worship and preaching. For all of us and for both churches, this was a significant change from the inherited 'the rector does all' model.

Although non-stipendiary from the diocesan perspective, I began to be paid by the church. Martin needed an administrator and, as it was relayed to me, someone suggested to Martin, 'Well, what about the chap with glasses. Surely he could do this?' So, it came to pass that I was appointed as administrator, initially on a half-day per week basis. As time went on, these hours were increased for a combination of administrative and pastoral reasons until, after a couple of years, I became a full-time member of staff. Part of my stipend came from the two churches and part came from a regional ministry called Living Water, about which I shall say more in Chapter 3.

By 1996, both parish churches had changed from being traditional Anglican churches to ones that were openly and confidently charismatic, with an increased openness to the renewing work of the Holy Spirit. The pace of change had been different in each church, but there had certainly been change in both – and the pace was set to increase yet again. The previous year a new wave of the Spirit, which became known as the Toronto Blessing,[35] had begun to spread around the world. It touched us too. We changed our pattern of services to enable us to make more space for the ministry of the Holy Spirit. Our morning services at the two parish churches were synchronised to start at the same time and, after preaching the Word, we would invite the Holy Spirit to come. The essence of this season was to wait upon God and give more time and space for people to receive from Him. So that's what we did. There were physical manifestations of the Holy Spirit at work. Some were more

[35] An outpouring of the Holy Spirit that became known as the Toronto Blessing (also called the Father's Blessing) because it started in the Toronto Airport Vineyard church (now known as Catch the Fire) in 1994.

comfortable lying on the floor as they were prayed for under the power of the Holy Spirit. Some were released into laughter; others wept.

Once again it was all too much for some, but for others it was a season of new life and growth. Once again we needed to make time and space to explain what God seemed to be doing. Once again there were difficult conversations. By now, however, a head of steam had been built up and the train called 'renewal' was moving forward, especially so at St Nicholas', where the congregation had grown to be more than 100, including children and young people. There was a desire to create more space and flexibility within the building to facilitate greater freedom in our worship – to give space for prayer ministry and hospitality and to have the flexibility for all ages to meet together. There was also a growing realisation of the gap between the way we did church and the picture presented in the New Testament. There was a growing hunger to make the gospel more accessible to those who did not yet have a relationship with Jesus.

In order to use the space in the church building at Ashill more creatively, we wanted to be able to move the furniture. A plan to remove some of the pews in the south aisle was making progress through various committees and had the support of the majority of the church council. However, when the plans became known locally, a campaign was launched in opposition. Suddenly we found ourselves and our story not just making the regional news but on the pages of the national press, local radio and regional television. It was more than a local story. In fact, our story was a microcosm of a bigger one – one that illustrated a growing tension between traditional church and new forms of church formed either through a desire to express worship in fresh ways or to engage in mission and evangelism. This tension was exacerbated in village communities like our own, with more fixed, traditional expectations.

It became clear that any attempt to change the church furniture or furnishings would be a long and painful process. A few weeks before this exploded into the public domain, Martin and I had sensed God speaking through Isaiah 43:19: 'See, I am doing a new thing! Now it springs up; do you not perceive it?' We had both preached about this on consecutive Sundays. At the time, I don't think we were quite sure how this would be worked out, but we did know that God was up to something, that it would be significant and, by definition, something that we hadn't seen before. After all, it was going to be 'new'! There was a challenge from the preceding verse ('Forget the former things; do not dwell on the past', v18) that in order to take hold of the new we had to let go of the old, and a promise that as we did so, the Lord of the church would make a 'way in the wilderness' for the 'new thing' to flourish (v19).

At the time it felt like living in a pressure cooker. The momentum for change was irresistible, and it was only a matter of time before the pressure valve would need to be released. In the end it was Martin who pressed the release button. He took the view that as the route of reordering the medieval church building was proving difficult and raising hostility, it would be better to take the people elsewhere. He hoped that separation would enable the traditional and the renewed church to coexist, side by side. The invitation was extended to those who felt called to pioneer and plant a new church to start meeting in the local community centre. The bishop agreed to the move, provided that a form of traditional service was held in both parish churches, which we were only too happy to continue to lead and resource.

So, on one Sunday morning in mid-July 1996, ninety men, women and children met together in Ashill Community Centre at the very first gathering of 'The New Thing that God is doing'.

It was a difficult birthing process. We had tried to keep all the carriages connected to the train, but in the end this proved impossible to achieve. As a result, our birthing was more difficult and indeed very different from how it might have been today. We were established when the language and permission-giving culture of Fresh Expressions was yet to be created. At the time there was no shared language to communicate in, few models to which to point, no experience to draw upon; there was pressure from the institution to conform and be squeezed into the mould of the traditional church building and culture. At times our language and attitude probably did not help. It is hard to steer a ship through uncharted waters and always be gentle and kind to those who are called to stay in the harbour.

Martin commented on that time:

> For some of those who left the parish church, the parting broke ties which went back a very long way. This was a village church in which some of the congregation had been baptised and married, where they had worshipped all their lives and their fathers before them. In many cases their ancestors were buried in the churchyard. This place *was* church for them.[36]

There was pain on both sides and it has taken time for some of those relationships to heal.

Few churches are renewed without tensions and conflict, and yet more disappointments, difficulties and disagreements were awaiting us in the future.

What is it that causes opposition to renewal? Perhaps there are three most common factors.

First, and probably most significant of all, is the spiritual battle involved in contending for the King and His kingdom. Spiritual renewal isn't about the modernisation of the Church. It's a recognition of the need to be filled with the Spirit of God and a radical openness to whatever God has to give or wants to do. Jesus Himself experienced and promised conflict.[37] His followers can expect nothing less. It doesn't make it any less painful, but it helps us to see beyond the person who seems to be against us. As the apostle Paul said, 'For our struggle is not against flesh and blood, but against the rulers, against the

---

[36] Down, *Building a New Church Alongside the Old*, p37.
[37] John 16:33: 'In this world you will have trouble.'

authorities, against the powers of this dark world and against the spiritual forces of evil in the heavenly realms' (Ephesians 6:12).

At the height of the press coverage, my father and I were at opposite ends of the spectrum. He was churchwarden at St George's and I was very much associated with The New Thing. One of the Sunday nationals in particular attempted to capitalise on this, and I think we did a good job of not allowing that to happen. But obviously there were tensions. We each simply had to get on with being in the place we felt God was calling us to be, and leave it with Jesus to decide how and where to build His Church.

Second, the issue of traditionalism. We know this takes root when we focus inwards on church, our liturgy and services, above what God is calling us into, or above the need to engage in reaching out to others in mission. We have valued the rites and practices of our Anglican liturgical roots and found creative ways of honouring our heritage in the rhythm of our worship practice. But the problem of traditionalism arises when the attention of people and their worship is focused on these rather than on God Himself. As Jesus said, there will be those who prioritise 'human traditions' above 'the commands of God' (Mark 7:8). Often it's to do with our way of doing things: the music we play, the songs we sing, the language we use.

Incidentally, it's not restricted to issues of 'ancient or modern' – traditions are formed surprisingly quickly. We can all too easily become used to a comfortable, familiar format. In our case, we sometimes created problems for ourselves by changing too many things at the same time. It is hard to manage the tension between those who want nothing to change and those who want everything to change all at once. However hard we try, though, sooner or later there is likely to be one change too many for some.

Third, the issue of conservation. Each historic renewal of the Church has affected the way church buildings have been ordered. As Martin said at the time:

> Like its predecessors, this revival is leading to a desire to renew the physical surroundings of the church's work and worship. In the story of our own parish church, it was at this point that the irresistible force of spiritual renewal met an immovable object: the rock of modern conservationism.[38]

Occupying a building of historical or architectural interest often means that we have to live with a conflict between the values of the kingdom of God and the values of conservation. It is possible to reconcile these values, but when our buildings are not serving and helping to meet the mission strategy of the church, it is time to lock the door and pass the key on to those with a heritage concern. It was this issue of conservation, at least on the surface, that caused us to leave the traditional church building behind and move into the community centre.

Jesus often had to address issues of fear and doubt in His disciples. I suspect that most of us who are seeking to pioneer kingdom initiatives have to contend with these responses at times. I know that I certainly have. It can be the fear of failing, the fear of 'what if', the fear of simply not being able enough, the fear of change; fears that are often rooted in insecurity and inadequacy. For ourselves, we didn't know how this would turn out but we did believe that we were taking the right step. It was a time of change and challenge for us all, and some left our churches preferring to worship elsewhere.

There were, though, two unifying purposes that lay behind the formation of The New Thing. The first was connected to mission and the second to the practice of being church. We had a desire to reach with the gospel those not already in church. In the immediate aftermath of the new congregation being formed, we did find people joining the church. Some came from our own villages who had not been part of the parish churches; others were attracted from further afield. Some found faith for the first time and came from an unchurched background; others

---

[38] Down, *Building a New Church Alongside the Old*, p94.

had once been churchgoers but had not been back to church for some time. In terms of the practice of being church, we found a new freedom in our worship, prayer and meeting together, and we shall explore what this looks like and how it developed in ensuing chapters.

The renewal of the Church is always dependent upon personal renewal. There is no renewal of the Church without it. The stories of our personal experience of God at work in our lives are powerful. It's hard to argue with what God has done in someone's life. So let me bring this chapter to a conclusion with the story of just one person whose life was dramatically touched by God during this period.

Jean had attended a diocesan Day of Renewal back in 1989. At the end of the day the visiting speaker, David Pytches, had invited God to send the Holy Spirit. Jean had been afraid to let go and surrender her life to Jesus. David invited people to do just that with the words of Jesus, 'Come to me, all you who are weary and burdened, and I will give you rest' (Matthew 11:28). Jean went forward and asked Jesus into her life and to fill her with His Spirit – which of course He did. Martin tells the story:

> Unknown to anyone, she had been a manic-depressive for nearly thirty years. Moods of black despair and unbearable depression had alternated with times of whirling, uncontrollable mental activity. Her illness had first been diagnosed following two suicide attempts at the age of twenty-one. She had dropped out of college, unable to cope. In spite of this she had later met and married John and had brought up two children. For years she had been stabilised by heavy doses of lithium salts and anti-depressants prescribed by the doctor ... At the Day of Renewal something changed. She did not receive any prayer for healing but the Holy Spirit coming in and filling her soul gave her a new centre of peace.[39]

---

[39] Down, *Speak to These Bones*, p87.

There was more work God wanted to do in Jean's life. Later that year, she attended New Wine and was reminded of some very painful memories. She chose to forgive those who had hurt her and, on the final night of her time away, asked Jesus to heal her hurt and give her His peace. 'Suddenly she felt herself being bathed in lovely warm water, flooding through her whole body from top to toe, washing and cleansing every part of her.'[40]

Three years later, in 1992, at a similar event Jean was suffering from menopausal symptoms and went forward for prayer, seeking God's help. This time those praying for her sensed the presence of an evil spirit.[41] They prayed for the spirit to go and Jean returned a little shaken but conscious that something had gone. The following day, Jean seriously damaged her back and Martin and Maureen visited her in hospital. During their time with Jean, they discussed what had happened the day before. As they talked together, Jean was reminded of a childhood memory when she was twelve. 'Her parents had been shouting and fighting over the meal table and Jean had taken a knife to her throat. "If you don't stop", she had screamed at them, "I'm going to kill myself."'[42] They didn't and neither did she, but it seemed to be that moment that had given the opportunity for an evil spirit to come in. Martin and Maureen prayed with Jean, asking Jesus to heal that memory and her back as well.

About thirty-six hours later, early in the morning, Jean was praying in her hospital bed when she felt Jesus Himself come and lay his hands on her back. Her pain went and later that day she was discharged from hospital,

---

[40] Ibid, p89.

[41] Jesus often encountered evil or unclean spirits in His ministry and always delivered the person from their influence. See for example Matthew 12:28; Mark 1:26; Luke 6:18, 8:29. He commissioned His disciples to do likewise. See Luke 9:1; 10:17.

[42] Down, *Speak to These Bones*, p90.

the doctor telling her that she had made a remarkable recovery. God had done it all.[43]

Five years ago, Jean moved to live near her daughter and she died at the end of 2020. I spoke to her earlier that year and asked her to reflect on the events I have just described, and her relationship with God since. Her immediate response was rooted in a verse from Joel (2:25) as she spoke about how she had seen the Lord restore 'the years the locusts have eaten' in her life over the previous thirty years. He continued to give her strength to cope with anything she had to face – including the loss of her husband two years before.

The call to Christ is a call to discipleship. It's a journey. There were many touched by the hand of God who still chose to walk away from His call. At the same time, there are many more stories of lives transformed that could be included here. That is the nature of kingdom growth. The parable of the sower (Matthew 13:1-23) is our encouragement: some may falter for various reasons but in others the seed will find a fertile home, take root and flourish.

These were formative years in laying the foundations for what was to come. The adventure had only just begun.

[43] Ibid, p91.

2
Our New Home

He named it Rehoboth, saying, 'Now the LORD has
given us room and we will flourish in the land.'
(Genesis 26:22)

The church was being renewed in the power of the Holy Spirit.
You will understand from some of the previous chapter that
there were many joys and encouragements, but it was also hard
and painful at times. Nevertheless, under the grace of God, we
continued to grow and within two years The New Thing needed
a larger home. Rather like the Israelites in the days of the
tabernacle,[44] we were a mobile people of God. So, in 1998, we
moved our Sunday gathering to a newly built community centre
in the neighbouring village of Saham Toney. This would prove
to be our Sunday 'home' for the next six years.

There was a growing sense that the new congregation was
not a temporary work of the Holy Spirit, and five issues began
to present themselves. The first was that it became clear we
needed a new and more permanent name. Our name had
become abbreviated to The New Thing,[45] but by definition even

---

[44] The tabernacle, also known as the Tent of Meeting, was designed to
move with the people (Numbers 1:51).
[45] As previously mentioned, we were first known as 'The New Thing
that God is doing'.

this had a sell-by date. We decided to hold a friendly competition within the church inviting people to come up with suggestions, and the 'Fountain of Life' was the name we decided upon. It did not sound very Anglican, but this was clarified by our strapline: 'a missionary congregation of the Church of England'. Mind you, not everyone reads the small print and we had some people worshipping with us for several months before they realised we were Anglican! They were worshipping with us more because they identified with our vision and values rather than our denominational identity.

The second issue was that it became clear we needed to invest in nurturing and expanding our growing youth work. One day in 1998, Martin (obviously an anointed name!) Spaul came over to see the vicar. He felt that God was calling him to give up his job in order to work with young people here. On the same day, his wife, Wendy, happened to pick up a prayer card at church which was all about trusting God. Martin had already been working voluntarily with our young people – indeed, in 1996 he and his new wife had spent their honeymoon with them at Soul Survivor![46]

Martin's sense of call seemed like the answer to our prayers, but there were at least two problems. The first was that there was no money for such a post. The second was that he had no visible qualifications or experience for the job. His was an unlikely background in agriculture and farming. Martin didn't tick the boxes of training and experience, but he did possess three qualities in abundance: he loved Jesus, had a passion to see young people reached with the gospel and was called by God.

At this stage, the Fountain of Life congregation was still legally under the authority of the PCC of St Nicholas' Church. Therefore, the matter was put on the next meeting's agenda, at which it was agreed to step out in faith and appoint Martin as

---

[46] Soul Survivor festivals ran from 1993 to 2019, gathering thousands of young people to worship Jesus each summer.

our first paid youth worker. This was on the understanding that the funds to do so would be provided by the Fountain of Life congregation. Martin found some part-time employment alongside his youth hours, and he and Wendy simply poured their hearts out into the youngsters, who blossomed in their care. Our own son, Simon, was discipled through his teenage years by this amazing couple, and they had a significant impact on his spiritual growth.

The third issue was the question of how all three 'churches'[47] would move forward together under one shared leadership. Since the formation of the new congregation in 1996, Martin Down had continued to be the rector of the two parish churches as well as the Fountain of Life. He was supported in this by Alan, who was a non-stipendiary minister, a licensed reader, Wendy Sargeant, and me. During this time we served all three churches, leading services, preaching and exercising pastoral care. We did our best to treat all three equally, but there was a perception, rightly or wrongly, that the Fountain of Life was Martin's priority. So a desire grew in the parish churches for separation from the Fountain of Life and for its own minister to be appointed. So it was that after much heart-searching, prayer and debate, Martin resigned as rector of the two parish churches on millennium eve, 31st December 1999, to be appointed from 1st January 2000 solely as leader of the Fountain of Life.

The rest of the licensed team were asked to decide where their commitment should be directed. Alan felt called to be a bridge-builder with the parish churches, I was licensed as a curate specifically to serve the Fountain of Life and Martin and I were joined by our reader, Wendy.

Martin continued to be paid a stipend by the diocese, but there was an additional issue of accommodation for Martin and Maureen to be resolved as the rectory would be needed for the

---

[47] At this stage the Fountain of Life had not been formally established as a church.

new incumbent of the parish churches. They therefore needed a house in which to live, and it really needed to be local. At this time, the diocese further demonstrated its generous commitment by agreeing to purchase a property, and Wendy and her husband, Jim, had the solution to the need for it to be local. They lived in Ashill and already had a plan in place that sometime in the future they would sell their house, retaining part of the original back garden in which they would build a bungalow for themselves. They fast-forwarded this plan, sold their house to the diocese and Martin and Maureen moved in.

So the separation was completed. It was not Martin's first choice, but it is what happened. A new incumbent was appointed to lead the two parish churches and the benefice was further expanded to include two others. On reflection, difficult as it was at the time, this process set the Fountain of Life free to grow.

As a result, however, the Fountain of Life was no longer under the governance of the PCC of St Nicholas' Church, and so a fourth issue emerged. We needed to establish our own legal structure and define our relationship to the diocese, and this is set out in Appendix One. It was important that we had a structure that was recognisably Anglican, and gave us the same standing as a parish church within the diocese. It's worth reflecting that we did not have many models to go on at this point – we were breaking new ground.

A set of protocols was also drawn up to define the nature of the Fountain of Life and in particular to set out how a 'network' church would work in practice alongside its parochial neighbours. The quotes that follow are drawn from that set of protocols.

Three important distinguishing marks of the Fountain of Life were noted. The first was that, as a missionary congregation of the Church of England, the Fountain held 'a charismatic doctrine of the baptism of the Holy Spirit, seeking to develop distinctive, alternative forms of worship and church life, with a view to making the church attractive and accessible to those who would otherwise be unchurched or unbelievers, especially in the younger generation'.

Second, the Fountain of Life was called to 'reach out to the unchurched and unbelievers through the networks of relationships which its members have with their neighbours at home, at work, and at leisure, with families and friends'. This, importantly, established the principle that the Fountain of Life was not formed or limited by parochial boundaries.

Third, 'the main thrust of the Fountain of Life is evangelism through personal contact, through worship, through the fellowship of the church community, through preaching and teaching, through the ministry of signs and wonders, and through works of mercy and service'.

There were some technical and pastoral issues to agree upon, with regard to the way in which the Fountain of Life worked this out within the Anglican fold, concerning membership, baptism, marriage and funerals, and these were also set out. As licensed clergy, we were expected to play a full part in the life of both Deanery Chapter[48] and synod.

In the protocol we also expressed our desire to be 'a catalyst in encouraging and enabling other churches to be mission orientated in their own way' and our hope 'to be able to resource other churches, offering any gifts or skills that they might have or develop'. The purpose of much of this was to give confidence to those around us that we would not seek to replace their function as the 'parish' church and make it clear that our intent was to be a blessing to other Christians and churches in the area.

Our relationship to the diocese was further defined by virtue of the relationship to the bishop that we held as ordained clergy. Over time, we explored various options for a stronger legal relationship, including a Bishops' Mission Order,[49] but it would

---

[48] Deanery Chapter is the gathering of local clergy to plan, pray and support one another.

[49] Bishops' Mission Orders were introduced in 2007 as a way in which a bishop may legalise a mission initiative within a parish or across parishes.

not be until 2017 that we were formally established as an extra-parochial place (EPP).[50]

From the beginning, the Fountain of Life has been expected to be fully self-supporting financially. We negotiated with the diocese a revised 'parish share'[51] which was initially set as the costs of our stipendiary minister(s), together with national insurance, pension contribution and housing costs plus 10 per cent of our giving. We felt that this was a more transparent way of calculating our quota than the diocesan system at the time, and it ensured that financially we were nett contributors to the diocese. In due time the diocese changed its way of calculating the share to a model that was closer to this one.

The fifth and final issue was that it had become increasingly clear that the Fountain of Life needed a home and a base to work from. Planting a church in a building that is used continuously for other activities has a number of drawbacks. The capacity to meet midweek is seriously inhibited. Setting up for Sunday worship week by week demands a huge cost in terms of time and energy. Everything has to be set up and taken down again at the end of the service. Teams of people were needed, and work began about ninety minutes before we were due to meet and for as long again afterwards. The sound system had to be put in place week by week, urns fetched and carried, materials for children and young people provided, refreshments organised, tables and chairs set out and much more besides. On top of that, all the equipment had to be stored off site. Even though these days were exciting ones to live through, the physical cost upon the team making it all happen behind the scenes was great.

---

[50] An EPP is a means of legalising within the Church of England a church that is assigned a geographical area outside the jurisdiction of any parish.

[51] A parish share is the financial contribution made by a parish church to the diocese to cover local and central costs, the bulk of which is the cost of the incumbent.

Wonderful as the community centre was, its meeting facilities were also limited, restricting the number of groups that we could have for children and young people. Our crèche met in the broom cupboard! Outside Sunday mornings there was no space for storage or offices and this was becoming an increasingly significant problem.

So there developed a growing vision and desire to have our own building. It felt like a contradiction in terms. We had just left a building, with all its restrictions and maintenance demands, and had been spending a considerable amount of time and effort in teaching and demonstrating that the Church is not about buildings but people. A new temple made up of 'living stones' (1 Peter 2:5) built on the cornerstone of the person of Jesus Christ and our shared faith in Him, standing on the shoulders of the apostles and prophets who have gone before us (see for example Ephesians 2:19-22). The church building may be the visible sign of 'Church' in a community but the 'real' Church in any community is not the building but those who know and love Jesus. Those of us who are 'Church' can be so exhausted looking after our buildings and the demands of keeping Sunday services going, that we have nothing left to give to those around us the rest of the time. We wanted to set the people free to be 'salt and light'[52] in their communities. How did this square with a building project? But life is full of paradox and God's ways and thoughts tend to be higher and greater than ours (Isaiah 55:9).

A farming member of our church family offered us an acre of land upon which to build, if we could gain planning permission. We imagined that this was the answer to our need. However, our planning application failed. We appealed and a barrister specialising in planning law agreed to represent us pro bono. The appeal failed. However, the appeal process did

---

[52] See Matthew 5:13-16 where Jesus is teaching His disciples and calls them to act as salt and light in the world around them by showing the unconditional love of God in word and deed.

establish as a legal principle the need we had for a worship centre in Ashill should appropriate land become available. This seemed to reinforce a prophetic word that had been spoken over the church in the past. Rooted in our history was a promise that seemed to be connected to our presence in Ashill from Matthew 5:14: 'A city on a hill cannot be hidden.'[53] So we waited to see what God would do.

Three days later the owner of a business in the village offered us first refusal on purchasing his property, which included land, a workshop and his home. He had decided to sell up and, although he didn't believe in God, felt that He wanted him to offer us first refusal! However, he needed the church to give him an immediate decision and that required the not insignificant matter of needing £250,000 to purchase the property.

Preliminary enquiries of the local planning department indicated that change of use would be permitted. So, the following Sunday the congregation – by now about ninety adults – was given the opportunity to respond. The total given or pledged on that one day in August 2000 was an extraordinary £292,000. Not only did this enable us to purchase the property, but it also left enough finance to begin drawing up plans and converting the bungalow for office and meeting-room space. Planning permission was granted and building work commenced. Eventually the development of the site and the building of a 250-seat worship centre was completed, at a total cost of £750,000. We took out a mortgage of £160,000 but the rest of the money was freely and sacrificially given by members of the Fountain of Life family.

Just as God provided creative craftsmen like Bezalel and Oholiab to furnish the tabernacle (Exodus 36:1), He also raised up for us an army of practically gifted people to complete the worship centre. Lionel was a professional BBC sound engineer who worshipped with us during our time in the community

---

53 NIV 1984.

centres. He led a small team in the weekly labour of setting up the PA system. He specified equipment, mapped the wiring diagram and took the lead in installation. Paul was a landscape gardener with training as a tree surgeon and he designed the planting and landscaping on the site. We had a wonderful team of professional builders who, although not members of our church, at times exhibited more faith than we did!

From the beginning we felt it was important to establish that the building project and its ongoing maintenance were separate from the mission of the people of God who occupy the building. We are sojourners, tenants, passing through, not shaped or limited by the building. The building is our tabernacle or tent which, if necessary, we needed to have the freedom to leave behind. So a separate trust was established, called Cornerstone Building Trust (CBT). It had its own trustees and its responsibilities were to ensure the buildings were maintained, manage any further property acquisitions made, arrange the essential services and pay the running costs. CBT was the landlord; Fountain of Life and its related activities, the tenant. The trustees of CBT were appointed by the Fountain of Life board of trustees and served for five years although could be reappointed. This ensured that the building did not become disconnected from the purpose for which it was built, and left the trustees of the Fountain of Life free to focus on the people and its call to be missionary.

Throughout this period of the building project, the church continued to see sustained, gentle growth. Apart from Sundays, our pastoral and discipleship focus was through the small groups, which between us Martin and I would visit on an occasional basis. We encouraged each person to be in a home group and would allocate to a group for pastoral care those who for one reason or another could not physically attend a group. Meeting together in small groups is vital at any stage of a church's development and life, but was especially so during this period of having no other midweek meeting points. At this time some 80 per cent of our membership was connected to a small group.

In October 2004 we moved into our new worship centre. We were joined by our local bishop and, amid much celebration and thanksgiving, the site was dedicated to the glory of God and the extension of His kingdom. Having moved into our new premises, we needed a name for the site which marked the buildings as separate from the Fountain of Life. We did not want to lose the emphasis on the church being about people. Initially our 'working title' was Rehoboth, taken from Genesis 26:22 and the story of Isaac reopening the wells dug in the time of his father Abraham. After a few failed attempts, Isaac was able to open up one of them and 'named it Rehoboth, saying, "Now the LORD has given us room and we will flourish in the land."' Rehoboth spoke into our history and gave us promise and hope for the future. But we needed a name that spoke for itself rather than having to be explained. So, another competition! This time it was an eleven-year-old boy who came up with the name: The Well. Simple but profound. Wells attract, wells are the centre of a community, wells satisfy the thirsty, wells enable a land to be watered and Jesus had one of His most fruitful conversations with a woman at a well: a conversation that transformed her life and that of her community (John 4). Our call as a church was to redig the 'wells of salvation' (Isaiah 12:3) and be a source of living water in our local area. The title of this book reflects that call.

Four months later we had not just a new home but a new leader too. Earlier in 2004 Martin had announced his retirement, to be effective from February 2005. While this was not unexpected, there was much sadness about it too. Our church secretary at the time, Jean, summed up the feelings in an addendum to her report that year: 'Martin, we do not want you to retire. We love you. But your vibrant faith, passion for Jesus, teaching and leadership has clearly shown us how, like the man at the beginning of the year,[54] to put our hands into God's and face the future.' The future required a new leader.

What should happen next? The first question was: should I be the one to succeed him or should the church look elsewhere? At the time of my ordination there was an understanding that my designation as 'local' would always mean leading as part of a team, not as the incumbent of a church – and certainly not the church at which I had served as curate. However, since then, courtesy of our diocesan bishop, Graham James, my form of ordination had changed. Earlier, in 2002, I had been to see Bishop Graham and during our time together he felt that, in view of how my wider ministry had developed, it would be more appropriate for me to change my type of ordination from local to open. I would still be non-stipendiary as far as the diocese was concerned, but it would increase opportunities for me to minister more widely, and also open the door to my leading a church in the future. Bishop Graham had a wonderful ability to match people to situations and a wisdom and willingness to release what God was doing in different places, even if others around him did not quite get it. Many of my colleagues attest to his ability to listen, affirm and release them into God's purposes and plans.

He arranged for me to follow the standard procedure in such cases, which required me to meet with three separate individuals across the country. They were all in agreement and so the transfer was agreed, to take immediate effect.

Since that time, I had continued to serve full-time alongside Martin, who was of the view that either I should take over from him or be leading a church elsewhere. Bishop Graham agreed that there was a case for succession and confirmed that I could be a candidate for the position. Furthermore, he saw the need to ensure continuity by making an appointment before Martin formally retired.

---

[54] See the poem 'The Gate of the Year', by Minnie Louise Haskins (1875–1957).

My own view was that if everyone else was in agreement that I was the one to be appointed, then my answer would be 'yes'. So, what did the church think? A steering group was established to find out. It was chaired by our reader, Wendy.

All due procedures were followed and ultimately the question was put to the church, with each person voting in secret with the options 'yes' or 'no' as to whether they wanted me to be the one appointed. No middle ground – simply 'yes' or 'no'. In the event, their unanimous decision was – yes! The next step was for me to be interviewed by Bishop Graham and our new suffragan bishop, James Langstaff. They gave their permission and blessing. The continuity of leadership succession was assured. Not unique within the Church of England, but certainly at this time very much the exception to the rule.

Bishop Graham, our diocesan bishop between 1999 and 2019, was such a wise and strategic influence in our growth through this period, opening doors for us, speaking well of us and releasing us as a church – and me personally – into the things to which we felt called. We have much for which to thank him.

So here we were having experienced two momentous changes. We had just moved in to our new premises. Now we had a new leader too. There was much excitement and anticipation, but also a measure of uncertainty and questioning that comes with leadership transition.

We were at this stage about 125 adult members strong. Our facilities were much improved. We had a wonderful new worship centre, freshly painted, equipped with permanent lights and PA, new carpet and comfortable chairs. Our crèche could finally move out of the broom cupboard into a somewhat more appropriate location! The building work had absorbed the focus of our attention for the past three or four years. Now we needed to work out what we were here for, what the landscape might look like five or ten years down the line because we were here, and what our central purpose was.

It had been established that our calling was to be a missionary congregation of the Church of England. What did we need to do to be true to this calling? A healthy church is measured by its sending rather than seating capacity – but what did it look like to be a 'sent' church? In the New Testament, Church and mission are complementary terms. The outcome of mission is the Church, and without mission at the heart of its agenda the Church dies. But, what would it be like to be a church that was shaped by mission? In particular, what would that look like for us?

At the time I was reminded of Joshua who, having succeeded Moses, was the leader of the Israelites when they finally crossed the river Jordan to take possession of the land promised to Abraham. Just before crossing over, he gathered the people and told them to make sure they followed the ark of the covenant 'since you have never been this way before' (Joshua 3:4). He did not confess it but, of course, neither had he. We too were entering into new territory and no one quite knew what to expect, including me.

One of the most helpful prophetic pictures that we received at this time of transition was given by Julia, a long-standing member of the church. In the picture was a row of three seed trays containing mushroom compost. In the first tray there was plenty of compost but no mushrooms; in the second tray there were some mushrooms beginning to emerge; the third tray was overflowing with mushrooms. At that time we were in the second tray but with the promise of the third yet to come. An amazing picture, given that our past history hardly seemed barren or void. We had seen the hand of God at work in our midst. But this picture suggested that this was only the beginning.

Our understanding of the purpose of the prophetic in a leadership or strategic application is that it serves to affirm or confirm the direction the church is heading in rather than to take the place of leadership. The prophetic sits alongside the apostolic. In other words, follow the leader but expect the leader to make space to listen to what the Spirit is speaking prophetically. This picture seemed to be encouraging us that we were in step with His plan and set us up to receive the expansion of ministries and opportunities that were to follow.

At our first trustees' vision day in 2005 we began to drill down into the big questions of our identity, purpose and priorities. We began by defining our values. These included:

- placing ourselves under the authority of God's Word and the whole counsel of God as revealed in the Bible;
- prioritising the renewing power of the Holy Spirit;
- investing in the family of God as a place in which we become whole;
- growing intimacy in worship with the aim of encountering God;
- believing in the priesthood of all believers in which every member gets to exercise their gifts and ministries;
- committing to work across the generations in recognition of the capacity of all ages to meet with God.

We had high hopes. Our aspirations were to be a place where:

- the presence of God is tangible;
- people make friends easily;
- the wounded are made whole;
- new people are regularly coming to faith in Jesus and growing as His disciples;
- the potential of each person is realised;
- each person's gifts and talents are used to the glory of God;
- each person is equally valued.

We hoped the church would be a place that:

- is fun to belong to;

- excels in all that it does;
- reaches out to the wider community;
- embraces the poor.

At the heart of our vision has been a sense of call to present the gospel afresh in our generation. We were inspired by Isaiah 54:2 to 'enlarge the place of [our] tent', and interpreted this as an invitation, as well as a need, to grow a large, resourcing church to serve the local area.

In a rural area there is often an expectation that church will be small. Yet, God had already established something that was larger than the churches immediately around and we took this as a call to pursue numerical growth. Our missionary mandate required it. If our aspirations were to be met we knew that we needed the resource of people and the finance, gifts and ministries that come with them. In a rural area, we couldn't leave any area of ministry to 'the church down the road'. At that time, the local Anglican churches were struggling under the weight of the demands of parochial ministry, often inhibited by pressures of maintenance of buildings, and under-resourced in terms of clergy, finance and lay ministry resources, with a predominantly elderly congregation.

So, our vision was to grow and become a resource church in our area, which in turn would release others to grow around us. In order to fulfil this, our first target was to double in size. We began to imagine what it would look like to be a church of 250 adults. We prayed and we planned. It is said that you get what you pray for! But you also need to plan as if your prayers are going to be answered with a 'yes'.

Before we could move forward with our vision, we needed to take the opportunity afforded by new leadership, and, in the context of occupying a very visible and physical place of worship in the form of The Well, to clarify our relationship with other churches in our area, some of whom still felt uneasy about our existence. When the Fountain of Life was first established as an independent congregation, it was anticipated that a formal team ministry would be established encompassing the local market town, four villages and the Fountain of Life. In the end this structure did not come to pass, but it was still helpful for there to be a set of protocols that defined the basis for how the Fountain of Life would relate to the parish churches and vice versa. I was charged with drafting a covenant which would form the basis of this and also act as a guide for the relationship between the Fountain of Life and other parish churches in the diocese. It ensures that we take notice of the parish churches around us and also, importantly, vice versa. Its intention was to encourage mutual respect and foster a spirit of cooperation. You will find the text of this covenant in Appendix Two.

One evening a joint service was convened and I and the leaders of our neighbouring local parish churches, in the presence of the bishop and members of our churches, all signed the covenant.

There are still tensions at times in these relationships. Our presence changed the landscape. The Fountain of Life is the odd one out and we can be seen as a challenge to the status quo, even a threat. Some people have moved into the area and chosen to join the Fountain rather than attend their local parish church. Nonetheless, over the years I have enjoyed very supportive relationships with my fellow clergy, even if, at times, some have struggled with our existence. The parish system is under pressure in rural areas; some would say that it is no longer fit for purpose. Time will tell. It is clear, though, that at the very least, other models are needed. Our network church model is one of these.

Once again I'll bring this chapter to a close with some testimony. This time in the form of the story of how two couples journeyed to faith over the ensuing years.

First, the story of Ian and Victoria. In 2008, Victoria was invited by a friend to come along to Noah's Ark, our weekly parent and toddlers group. She began to make connections and friends, particularly with Andrea and Pippa. She came with her eighteen-month-old daughter, Olivia, and at Christmas they came along to our Family Fun time. Each time Victoria left Noah's Ark, Andrea would say, 'It's worship for all ages on Sunday.' Finally Victoria said to her partner, Ian, 'We really must go one Sunday.' They eventually did come one Sunday but it was not until the following year, 2009, that Victoria started coming regularly of her own volition. She met Fi, who started giving her various books by Nicky Gumbel.

One day, while reading one of these books, Victoria had a vision of Jesus extending His arm towards her and He seemed to be inviting her to, 'Come on through.' Victoria said 'yes', knowing somehow that Jesus was everything she had been searching for, and life just seemed to make more sense with Him in the picture. In January 2010 she attended Alpha and the pieces all began to fit together.

After Alpha the group decided to stay together, led by Pippa, and Victoria's faith continued to grow and her friendship circle in the church expanded. Meanwhile, to the joy of us all, she and Ian got married and I conducted their marriage blessing. Ian was somewhat reluctantly coming along to church to support Victoria. Then Ian ran into problems at work and financial difficulties, and this led to something of a Damascus Road experience for him.[55] It changed his outlook. Perhaps for the first time he had a season of soul-searching and a wilderness experience. He began to have conversations about faith, people prayed for his situation and things began to happen which he recognised as answers to prayer and evidence of a God who is real.

Ian then did the Alpha course himself, which helped him understand more, but he was still not convinced enough to fully surrender his life to Jesus. He needed further persuading. After all, Victoria had been given a clear sign – could God not do the same for him? In the end, Ian needed three signs to convince him! First, they needed a house, and Ian saw the hand of God

---

[55] See the story of Saul's conversion in Acts 9 as he was travelling to Damascus.

in the way that their new home was provided. It needed extensive renovation and this was a lesson for Ian in humility and a parable of the restoration he needed in his life. It was also a lot of hard work!

The second sign was connected to Victoria. At eight weeks pregnant, she was rushed to hospital with a rupturing ectopic pregnancy, a life-threatening condition. She had suffered an ectopic pregnancy previously in 2006 which had resulted in one of her fallopian tubes being removed. The surgeon explained that they would most likely have to remove her remaining fallopian tube. Victoria's friend Fi, who had taken her to hospital, asked the surgeon if she could pray for her and the surgeon was happy for her to do so. Victoria was taken to theatre and operated on immediately. When Victoria was conscious again, the surgeon came to see her and said, 'You have had a miracle. You can still have children!'

Against unimaginable odds, the pregnancy had become attached to a very tiny piece of fallopian tube left after the removal of her first ectopic pregnancy. This left her with a working tube and the chance of being able to conceive again.

The third sign came while Ian and Victoria attended the New Wine summer event. This gave Ian the intensity of encounter through both the worship and the Word that he was looking for and he met other people who spoke his language. This was the moment of conversion for Ian. He fully welcomed Jesus in. Then, at one of the evening sessions Ele Mumford[56] was speaking and gave a word[57] that she had been given about a couple who were attempting to conceive. This was for them. Encouraged by their friends, they went forward for prayer and were not satisfied until Ele had prayed for them personally.

Ian came back from New Wine and said to me, 'I'll get baptised if you can find me a river.' So we did, and in late August

<hr>

56 Ele (Eleanor) and John Mumford led the Vineyard churches in the UK and Ireland for more than twenty years until 2015.
57 As in, a prophetic word from God; see 1 Corinthians 14:6.

Ian was baptised in the river.[58] Their daughter, Tabatha, was born the following May – almost exactly nine months later, and six months after Ian and Victoria had been confirmed in Norwich Cathedral.

Ian and Victoria are still worshipping with us today and are committed to seeking God's plan for their lives. They often speak of how Jesus gives their life 'completeness'.

Rob and Helen are another wonderful story of God at work in drawing people to Himself. Rob finally succumbed to constant barraging from his sister and did Alpha in April 2007. He was settled at work but felt he had reached something of a crossroads in the overall direction and shape of his life. Having been brought up in a Christian home, he recognised lots of things through Alpha that he already knew, but his knowledge was somehow sharper and more clear than before. The turning point was on the Holy Spirit day. He describes himself as 'being filled with an absolute peace. There was a power that came across me. I'm used to playing rugby and used to being felled by power but this was a different type of power. It was a sensation of complete relaxation.' He started coming to church regularly.

Outside church Rob met Helen, a paediatric nurse, and on their first date he advised her that he went to church. She herself had just started going to church and the following year she too did Alpha with us. Helen made friends with Julia and asked her lots of questions. Helen recommitted her life to Jesus, was strengthened in her faith and saw answers to prayer as she prayed for the children she nursed.

Rob and Helen married in 2009 and now have three children. Helen was part of a team from the Fountain of Life that went on a mission trip to Uganda. Initially, she was rather reluctant to do this, feeling that everyone else had a clear role on the team except for her. By the time she returned, however, Helen felt reaffirmed in her calling to be a carer of others, the one who

---

[58] You can watch Ian's baptism at www.youtube.com/watch?v=L9Y-i9Z2Fkw (accessed 17th November 2020).

looks after people. She is now deputy ward sister on a paediatric ward. In the midst of the Covid-19 outbreak, I asked her what difference it made now to know Jesus. Her response was that it 'gives you hope and peace in uncertain times and helps you not to worry about things you cannot control'.

The greatest reward of any ministry is to see the mystery of God's grace at work in people's lives to bring revelation, transformation and redemption. These stories are illustrative of how God answered our prayers and called individuals into relationship with Him. We know that this only happens by the power of the Holy Spirit to the glory of God, but how exciting it is to work in partnership with the One who opens the eyes of the blind.

Having explored our context and formative years, in the following chapters we shall examine our life together by exploring particular aspects of our life and experience that have been significant to our growth. The first of these is how our partnership in the gospel with others has developed, and to tell this story we shall need to revisit our history, viewing it through this particular lens of the call to preserve the unity of the Spirit.

3
Come and Help Us

How good and pleasant it is
when God's people live together in unity!
... For there the LORD *bestows his blessing.*
(Psalm 133:1,3)

Luke sets the calling of the first disciples in the context of a fishing trip (Luke 5:1-11). On the shores of the Sea of Galilee, Simon Peter lends Jesus his boat for a sermon and, when He has finished, Jesus invites Peter, 'Put out into deep water, and let down the nets for a catch.' Jesus is a carpenter, not a fisherman. Peter is the one who knows how to fish. All of Peter's experience suggests that this is not the time for fishing. He's just returned from a fruitless all-night fishing expedition, his nets are drying in the sun and he's probably feeling exhausted. Yet, there is something about Jesus that causes Peter to act counterintuitively and say 'yes'. You kind of know how the story is going to end.

Jesus is in the boat, the fish can't wait to join Him and the nets begin to break under the strain of the huge number of fish caught. So Peter – and no doubt his brother Andrew – signal to their partners James and John to come and help them. Partnership is essential to the harvesting of fish and it's essential to the harvesting of souls. The kingdom is always bigger than any one church can contain. Some time ago I sensed the Holy

Spirit impressing upon me the phrase, 'Every movement of God needs the momentum of a mobilised people of God.' Together we can achieve more.

Personal and congregational renewal has always been our main focus. However, since the early days of seeing God at work in our churches, we have felt a call to equip, encourage and empower other churches too. I mentioned earlier that in 1993 we began to run the Alpha course. At that time, we were one of the first churches in Norfolk to do so. As a result we found that we were welcoming members of other churches to our Alpha course. They in turn began to invite others in their circles to come to subsequent courses, many of whom lived a fair distance away from our church. While a short-term commitment to do Alpha was sustainable, maintaining a long-term discipling relationship at distance was not, and nor did we want to primarily grow through transfer growth.

However, we did want to see more churches equipped to run Alpha for themselves and embrace the values that it enshrined. This would surely be more effective in seeing the kingdom come in Norfolk and would further empower Christians in other churches to be able to invite their friends to 'come and see'.[59] That's the beauty of Alpha: it releases us all to be effective witnesses by giving us a means of harvesting about which we can feel confident. All we need to do is extend an invitation. So we approached HTB and invited Nicky Gumbel, who was responsible for Alpha, and Sandy Millar, at that time the vicar of HTB, to hold a regional Alpha training conference in Norfolk. They said 'yes' and we organised it to take place in Norwich. We made it known to churches across Norfolk and, to our amazement, more than 300 attended. They were equipped and envisioned to take Alpha back to their local churches and many new courses began as a result.

---

[59] In John's Gospel, Philip invites Nathanael to 'Come and see' (1:46); Jesus invites Andrew and one other disciple to 'Come ... and you will see' (John 1:39); Andrew brought his brother Simon (Peter) to Jesus (John 1:42).

This also had an unexpected outcome for us. It increased our connection with other churches in the region, and in conversation with other leaders it became clear that there was a thirst for more regular opportunities to gather together. So, we began to invest in organising teaching and equipping days to encourage and build up the body of Christ in the region.

At one of these, towards the end of 1994, Martin Down invited David Parker, a church leader from the States who was at the time staying in the UK, to come and speak. He spoke on 'Mind the Gap' between Church and culture. The day itself bore much fruit but at this conference Martin sensed God saying, 'I want something bigger.' As he prayed into this more, the 'something bigger' clarified itself in his mind to be a three-day event, similar to a New Wine summer conference, held over a Bank Holiday weekend, which he believed should be called Living Water.

We had already received so much as a church from attending New Wine. We had taken people from our churches to its summer event each year since its formation and this group had grown from nine to sixty. Many lives had been changed and it had also helped to change our churches. It had given people a taste and thirst for singing the worship songs, applying the teaching and engaging in ministry in the power of the Spirit the rest of the year, not just at New Wine. It had been a significant part of our story and growth. But you had to be fairly committed to get to New Wine. It was held on the other side of the country in Shepton Mallet, some 250 miles away, lasted a full week in the summer holidays, and camping was not everyone's experience of 'heaven on earth'. Martin's vision for a three-day event would have all the ingredients of New Wine, with programmes for all ages, but be more accessible to people from our region. Most people in Norfolk could travel in on a day basis if they could not face the camping experience, and those further afield could come and camp or stay in local bed and breakfast or hotel accommodation.

We already knew from our conversations with local leaders that there was a growing desire within the county for leaders and churches to have opportunities during the year to gather together, to receive from leaders in other parts of the country and the world who could encourage us with the things that God was doing in their areas. Martin spoke to David Pytches, who was enthusiastic, and New Wine sowed financially into the first event with some start-up money. Others came forward to offer financial support. We discovered that the Royal Norfolk Showground near Norwich was available for the first Bank Holiday weekend in May. Martin knew that the Norwich Youth for Christ (NYFC)[60] organisation held its own May Day event for young people elsewhere in the city and was concerned not to have a competing event. However, Ian Savory, NYFC's director at the time, embraced the vision, agreed to work together with NYFC leading the youth programme, and Living Water was born.

Trustees were appointed and we also formed an executive to be the leadership team drawn from across churches in the region. Becky, who had worshipped at St Nicholas' before going to university and had just returned having completed a degree in business studies, was appointed as the first administrator. Programmes were organised for all ages. With a budget of more than £100,000 and a team of volunteers numbering 250, the needs were significant, but God was in it, and at the end of nearly two years of planning, 'finally the day dawned. In the adult venue (appropriately the Sheep Pavilion) the seats filled up, the lights came on; we welcomed the people, about a quarter of who were at an event of this sort for the very first time'.[61] About 1,200 men, women, young people and children attended the first event in 1996.

It felt as if God's favour was upon us and our influence within the region continued to grow and develop. Many more

---

[60] www.norwichyfc.co.uk (accessed 25th January 2021).
[61] Down, *Streams of Living Water*, p115.

churches were running Alpha, and Pippa and I were leading the team to coordinate this in Norfolk. In 1999 we attended an Alpha leaders' event at HTB, at which we heard that the international evangelist, speaker and author J.John[62] had developed a mission series called Just 10. This series expanded the teaching of the Ten Commandments and applied each one to day-to-day living in a positive way. J.John was looking for places where there was a partnership of churches and a vision for equipping the local church in personal evangelism. It had borne much fruit elsewhere and the connections we had with churches through Living Water gave us the opportunity to explore whether there was sufficient support to justify inviting J.John to Norfolk. We organised a leaders' meeting and about forty attended to hear J.John outline how it would work. Those who came were all in enthusiastic support, and some agreed to form the basis of a steering group for the series. Living Water trustees agreed to be the covering organisation for the mission in Norfolk and I agreed to chair the steering group of about twenty people. I grossly underestimated the size of this undertaking. In the end, 138 churches took part and the budget grew exponentially to £145,000.

In order to launch the series, we held an evangelistic event at Christmas in Norwich Cathedral. Participating churches were asked to restrict attendance to those who were bringing a guest with them. Even so, it became very clear that the cathedral would be too small for the number we knew were coming. We had to come up with a solution. It was one of those few occasions when my sleep was disturbed until I sensed the Holy Spirit giving me a couple of names to talk to about it the following day, reminding me that it was not my burden to carry alone. Sure enough, those conversations provided the solution in the form of an additional marquee and we trusted the God who provides for the money to cover this unexpected cost.

---

[62] For further information on J.John and the ministry of Philo Trust, see canonjjohn.com/ (accessed 25th January 2021).

Despite this additional space we still had to turn people away, but it was a hugely encouraging start.

The Just 10 series itself took place over ten weekly evenings in the summer of 2002. Each week we met on a Wednesday evening in the Sheep Pavilion at the Royal Norfolk Showground – the same venue as the one used by Living Water for its adults' programme. Each week for the ten-week duration some 3,000 people gathered. There was a regular response each week of more than 300 either making first-time commitments to follow Christ or recommitting their lives to Him, and many more coming forward for prayer about the particular issues raised. During the event, amnesty bins were provided so that people could safely hand in dangerous items such as knives, guns and other weapons. On another occasions those present were invited to return stolen goods and, if it was not possible to return them to their original owners, they could use the amnesty bins for this purpose. The bins were overflowing with countless library books, hotel towels, jewellery and even cash – the proceeds of which were given to charity.

It was a huge effort and demanded a huge task force drawn from churches across the region. Our music team rose to the occasion and headed up worship and our technical team headed up the sound and visuals.

Our church did not directly grow numerically through our involvement in this mission, but it did give us opportunities to foster unity and partnership with others. It involved a lot of people from our church on teams, and it always develops the muscle of the local church to be involved in events larger than itself. The Fountain of Life has often been described as a church that punches above its weight. This was another opportunity to do just that.

Meanwhile, Living Water continued to be held as an annual event. It moved from the May Bank Holiday weekend to a full week during the summer holidays. Excellent programmes were provided for children and young people. Attendance grew to about 3,000. Over the years of its life, Living Water played such a significant part in releasing initiatives and encouraging leaders and churches in the region. For many it would be the first event to be entered on their calendar. Living Water was a real place of transformation, inspiration and encouragement for many. Despite its success, however, it had been necessary most years for a substantial offering to be taken to cover the shortfall of running the event. When New Wine, out of which Living Water had been planted, moved its regional event for the north from Harrogate to Newark, within touching distance of East Anglia, it seemed to be an opportunity to pool our resources. In 2005 the trustees of Living Water decided that the following year would be the last Living Water event. It was a decision received with a mixture of understanding, sorrow and disappointment. But it is as important to hear the Lord say 'stop' as it is to motor on through the green lights. At the time, I sensed the Spirit was saying that the closure of Living Water would be like taking out a large tree – there would be lots of shoots of new growth that would emerge as a result.

The first of these for us occurred in 2007 when we introduced the Mission-Shaped Ministry[63] course to the diocese. This had been developed by the Fresh Expressions team to equip those with a vision and call to start new forms of church or revitalise existing ones. We spent time in consultation with the bishop's staff and received their support to host the course on their behalf in partnership with the Methodist church. It was attended by around fifty people from churches across the diocese.

'The Father's Heart' weekend was another shoot of new life. We hosted the first one in 2010. The vision for it embraced some of the aims of Living Water but at a more local, though still regional, level. We hosted it on our church site; camping was available on a caravan park that was owned by members of

---

[63] Mission-Shaped Ministry is a one-year part-time course that equips, resources and supports pioneers and church planters. See freshexpressions.org.uk/resources-3/mission-shaped-ministry (accessed 25th January 2021).

our church and conveniently situated opposite the church. We partnered again with Norwich Youth for Christ to provide the youth work, our own church teams led the children's work and there was a teaching and ministry programme for adults. Financially it was much more sustainable and we were full to overflowing. This became a regular biennial event.

At the first of these in 2010, we launched another 'shoot': the Fountain Network. At its heart was a desire to connect individuals and churches who shared a vision for engaging in mission and rural evangelism locally. It gave a means by which churches could more purposefully partner together. Here are some stories of how the network worked and of the leaders it resourced.

Helen was a founding member of the network. She was appointed as vicar of a local Anglican church, Cloverfield, which was an existing church plant on an estate in Thetford – a town about fourteen miles to the south of us. At the time she felt the Lord saying that she should connect to the Fountain of Life. So, shortly after she moved into the area, she made contact with us. We provided prayer support and some worship team to encourage the raising up of others from her growing congregation. There were day conferences and resources that equipped members of her church in particular ministries, especially that of healing and the prophetic. Members of her church regularly attended our Sunday evening services for teaching and worship. Helen also belonged to a New Wine network group for leaders led by Pippa and me. This provided an opportunity for leaders connected to New Wine to meet together, pray, share lives, eat together and be encouraged. It's a form of accountability and an expression of partnership. This was a source of strength, encouragement and empowering for Helen:

> The relationship that we were able to establish with FoL was of great value for me personally – support in ministry, encouragement and a place to be fed and filled!

– and also had a significant impact upon the Cloverfield congregation.

Adam Jackson was involved in various projects which he wanted to position under the umbrella of the Fountain Network – in particular, his ministry with young people through an event called Intents.[64] Intents grew out of a Youth Alpha weekend which Adam ran in 2009 for the Fountain of Life's young people. The following year he invited youth groups from other churches in our local area to join our own young people at Intents. It took place over the second Bank Holiday weekend in May and was held at Adam's mother's farm which had several acres of land suitable as a temporary campsite.

This event seemed to fulfil a prophetic word that there would be a powerful move of God on the farm resulting in young people coming to faith. Here are some quotes from young people who attended that first event:

> It's been such a great experience which has really strengthened my relationship with God.

> When I was prayed for I started crying. Not because I was upset but because I was happy to be giving my life to Jesus.

> God showed Himself to me and I didn't feel as alone or empty as I had felt.

Intents went on to become an annual regional event for young people aged eleven to fourteen who either came on their own or with their church youth group for an extended weekend of teaching, worship and ministry. Youth groups from churches across the county and beyond came along to it. For a season, Urban Saints, formerly Crusaders, recommended it as an event

---

[64] This had begun during Adam's time as our youth worker, which I shall expand in Chapter 5.

for young people in the east. Intents had grown beyond the Fountain of Life. It needed its own identity and structure but still wanted to relate to the Fountain as its home. Fountain Network was the obvious place of belonging.

Jill had set up an organisation called 'Call to Prayer'.[65] Our relationship with Jill began when she became leader of the team of intercessors praying for the Living Water event. It developed further when she took on responsibility for organising prayer for the Just 10 mission. She had a vision for setting up 100 Lighthouses of Prayer across Norfolk who would meet monthly to pray for the Just 10 mission. In the end, 103 lighthouses were established. Many of these continued after the event and, at the time of writing, she has just relaunched the 'Lighthouse' concept across Norfolk as a response to the needs generated by Covid-19. Jill is committed to teaching, training and equipping the body of Christ in intercession, the prophetic and personal healing ministry. The Fountain Network was a natural spiritual home for her work. Jill comments:

> For us it has been a natural connection to work with the Fountain Network and linking in with Stephen during Living Water and Just 10 enabled us to grow as a ministry. The benefit of linking together and standing in unity to further the kingdom of God is really powerful, and causes us to grow in faith and friendship. Together we can do so much more.

Madeline was another founding member of this network. She was priest in charge at St Helen's Bishopgate in the city of Norwich. Two years earlier, in 2008, Madeline gave me a call and asked if we as a church would come and help her start a 'charismatic' congregation at her church. I had often mused on the strategic potential for a relationship between a resource church deep in rural Norfolk and one based in the city. This

---

[65] call2prayer.co.uk.

wasn't that but maybe this would be the beginning. So we said 'yes' and began to build a connection.

It was a bit of an odd place to imagine beginning such a congregation. Although St Helen's was located in the city, its primary purpose was to serve the needs of an elderly community living in accommodation provided by a charitable trust set up by the church. The congregation was largely made up from this residential community. But we had a close relationship with Madeline, who had served on placement with us during her training. So we agreed to give it a go and see what happened. We started by holding an evening 'charismatic' service in her church once a month on a Sunday evening. Madeline provided the space and the time; we provided the resources of people and equipment. Her daughter Chloe was instrumental in encouraging some younger adults to come along and the congregation experienced numerical growth. God was at work. On one occasion, Pippa sensed that God wanted to heal cataracts. An elderly lady responded and Pippa prayed for her and then asked her if anything had changed. The lady opened her eyes, which grew in wonder as she discovered that she was now able to clearly read the words on the screen.

Within a couple of years Madeline was appointed as incumbent of another church, St Stephen's, also in Norwich. This was a church much more prominently situated on a main thoroughfare connecting the city centre to a major indoor shopping centre. There could not have been a more strategic position in the city and this church had a rich heritage and reputation in the ministry of healing. At Madeline's licensing service, the bishop preached and made reference to the fact that Madeline would bring with her a charismatic service run in partnership with the Fountain of Life.

On the day of Madeline's installation, one of the walls in the chancel area cracked from top to bottom. It transpired that a water leak nearby had undermined the foundations of the church. It caused serious instability and the church was declared unsafe until remedial work (largely at the expense of the water company involved) was carried out. This proved to be a huge blessing. It enabled a major refurbishment programme to be completed as part of the building programme. Pews were removed and replaced by more comfortable and moveable chairs. The heating system was replaced. Kitchen facilities, toilets and office accommodation were all added. The funding for this project was filled with the unexpected provision of God through a myriad of different sources and people. A church fit for the twenty-first century emerged.

While all this work was going on, which took four years, all services were held in a nearby church hall. Some members of the St Helen's congregation had transferred with Madeline to St Stephen's. The church began to grow as people from elsewhere felt called by God to join. We continued to provide worship team, youth team and speakers. Slowly but surely, local team began to emerge. Alpha courses were held regularly and new people came to faith one by one.

Upon the return to the restored and refurbished church building, our direct involvement in its running diminished as more people were released into leadership from within. Our relationship with the church remained strong but changed. Adam, referred to earlier, had resigned from his position as our youth worker in order to move with his wife into the city to work alongside Madeline in growing a younger constituent in the congregation. He had already run youth activities at St Stephen's and had also taken teams from the Fountain to Norwich to engage with the homeless and pray for people on the streets. His work with the young adults over the previous few years has resulted in the unexpected fruit of four people under the age of thirty being called to ordination in the Church of England.

Members of our church who were living in or near the city joined the church. The congregation continued to grow, and a dedicated worship team began to emerge, as did other supporting leadership, eventually leading to additional ordained staff. St Stephen's has its own vision and life. It has a heart and a passion for reaching out to the marginalised, the poor and the homeless. It now has one of the best city-based cafés engaged in practical outreach.

Our partnership together hasn't developed in the way that I might have imagined in the beginning. Church planting and multiplication comes in all shapes and sizes. In church planting terminology, this partnership combined two entities so that they grew as one. It was a type of graft. Grafting is a term borrowed from gardening terminology used to describe the process of joining two plants into one. It takes a bud or shoot from one plant and grafts it in to grow on the stock of another. A new, healthy plant is formed which carries the DNA of both. In our particular context this involved the grafting of a small team which had its roots in the Fountain of Life into the ministry of St Stephen's in a way that produced renewal and new life.

This graft created a church that has its own unique form, shape and life. Over the course of time, our role has changed and the relationship between our two churches increasingly has had a greater mutuality. In some of our activities we are supporting each other. We have partnered in providing courses of biblical study in the city. We have partnered together in hosting events. We still consider ourselves to have a special bond with one another as 'sister' churches, and the Fountain Network has been a natural place of belonging that recognises this. But the original hope of a resource church in the city twinned with one in rural Norfolk has not yet been fulfilled.

It really doesn't matter that we seem to have ended up with a slightly different outcome. The kingdom has advanced and that really is the most significant outcome of all. What matters more is our faithfulness to step into the things we discern the Spirit is leading us into and allowing Him to shape it as we go. It's the fruit of allowing God to shape the church His way.

Recently I had a reminder that God is also at work in the journey – not just waiting at the destination. About six months ago, Pippa and I bumped into James while walking the North Norfolk Coast path. James responded to an invitation given during one of those early services at St Helen's and renewed his commitment to Jesus. At the time he was working for the Football Association in Norfolk. In 2018 he became a resident member in the fourth intake of the Archbishop of Canterbury's St Anselm Community for young people before serving on the Church of England's national Evangelism and Discipleship team, working with Fresh Expressions. He is now an ordinand studying theology at Ridley Hall.

All of this is illustrative of how in our history we have consistently positioned ourselves as a place of equipping and resource. There are many ways in which we have partnered with New Wine over the years as a hub and resource church. In 2018 our role as a resource church for the diocese was formally recognised by the bishop and we were appointed to serve in this way. At the beginning of 2020, we were hosting the diocesan Church Planting and Revitalisation course before Covid-19 stopped this in its tracks.

While it remains to be seen exactly how our role as a resource church develops, it is already clear that we have moved a long way from the starting point in our relationship to the diocese. Once very much on the fringe, a provocative voice at the margins, even perhaps at the beginning in danger of being excluded altogether, we have now moved to occupying a central role in mission and seeing the kingdom come.

This wider dimension to our story of equipping and resourcing others to see the kingdom come is intrinsic to our sense of vision and call and has shaped our life together. In the chapters that follow we shall look at how other priorities and values have been worked out in the family that is known as the Fountain of Life.

4
A Growing Family

I kneel before the Father, from whom every family in
heaven and on earth derives its name.
(Ephesians 3:14-15)

Pippa and I recently enjoyed a meal at an Indian restaurant. We were welcomed and escorted to our table. The restaurant was very full with a buzz of conversation. We noticed the way in which the restaurant owner marshalled their staff, gently directing them as necessary from behind the scenes. But it was the owner's attitude to their customers that particularly caught our attention. They greeted people as they arrived and said goodbye as they left. Some, like us, were there for the first time and we received a friendly handshake. Others, though, were regulars and some of these were greeted with a hug. One person had recently come home after an operation and received two hugs! Later on, the owner went one stage further and invited the person to come and see them at home. It was clear that the owner had a vision for running more than a restaurant. It felt like family.

'What does church mean to you?' I asked Andy, who heads up our sound and visuals team.

'It's my family,' came his instant reply.

Karen, who now serves as our church administrator, visited the Fountain of Life one Sunday morning. She recalls:

Stephen said to me, 'You're looking for a family.' He hit the nail on the head. After twenty years away from the UK I had not quickly found a church to call home and settle into. The people were friendly, open-hearted in their hospitality and genuinely excited about their faith in Jesus and all that God was doing. I'm so thankful to be part of what God is doing in this special family.

One Sunday morning I asked the congregation what they considered to be the vision of the church. The most moving and unexpected answer came from someone I recollect as saying that it was to build a church that shy people could feel at home in. This was from a person who months earlier found it impossible to leave their home. Then a Christian befriended them, invited them to Alpha and they discovered Jesus. Now, this person was standing and speaking in the midst of a congregation, most of whom they still did not know.

James and his mum started coming along to the Fountain in 1999, when James was aged four. He worked his way through all our children's and youth groups before eventually setting off for university. As a child, he was quite shy. Recently, his mum, Jo, a single parent, remembered saying to James as a teenager that she was concerned about the fathering deficit in his life. He replied, 'Don't worry, Mum. I have had plenty of father figures at the Fountain of Life.'

Family lies at the heart of what it means to be church. It's implicit in Jesus' teaching (Luke 8:21) and, although directly used sparingly in the New Testament (eg Galatians 6:10; Ephesians 3:15), is fundamental to our understanding of what it means to be church. We know that being sons and daughters of the King embraces this high calling to live as brothers and sisters to one another, building a community founded on love. Without love we are but 'a resounding gong or a clanging cymbal' (1 Corinthians 13:1). Jesus commands us to 'love one another' (John 13:34). It's a command with the key to its fulfilment given in the same verse: 'As I have loved you, so you must love ...' This is more than a model – it's the promise of empowerment as we allow ourselves to be loved by God. Loving one another involves us in being 'kind and compassionate' (Ephesians 4:32); being 'patient, bearing with one another in love' (Ephesians 4:2); serving one another (Galatians 5:13), accepting one another (Romans 15:7) and so much more.

The Fountain of Life has always worked hard at being known as a community with that kind of intentional, sacrificial love for one another. It is a love that heals us and makes us whole. It's a love that serves as our most effective witness to those outside the Church. This sense of being a loving community is probably the one comment that is reflected back to us more than any other by new people. It permeates the welcome given to visitors and newcomers; it generates a spirit of hospitality, acceptance and forgiveness.

One of the expectations we set out for new members is that they would forgive others readily. So often the Church is but a mirror copy of the world around us. Yet we are called to be 'salt' and 'light'[66] in our community, showing a better way for getting along with each other, 'preferring one another' (Romans 12:10, KJV) and genuinely caring for one another.

Clive was someone I first met in 1991 through my work with people facing employment difficulties. Following that time we maintained a friendship but, although his wife, Julie, had come to faith and worshipped with us, he remained a firm agnostic. He could understand there being a 'higher power' but, as Julie puts it, 'found it hard to accept the love of God, and loving God as Daddy (*Abba*) he found ridiculous as he was not a child'.[67] The concept of Jesus as being the only way to fully experiencing

---

[66] Matthew 5:13-16.

[67] *Abba* is an Aramaic word for 'father', demonstrating the intimacy and closeness Jesus experienced in His relationship to the Father (Matthew 11:25; Mark 14:36). By the (Holy) Spirit we are invited into the same depth of experience as we too cry, '*Abba*, Father' (Romans 8:15; Galatians 4:6).

the love of God was also a stumbling block.[68] Over the years, we had regular circular conversations about it all but he remained unmoved. Then he was diagnosed with mesothelioma[69] and became seriously ill. Various members of the Fountain of Life family gathered around Clive and Julie, offering practical support and simply loving them. I am quite sure that it was receiving the love of the saints – the people of God – that swept Clive into making a decision to invite Jesus into his life. It enabled him to understand something of the nature of God and His love for him and overcame his intellectual blockages. He worshipped with us regularly until his condition worsened and, one day, Clive received the news that his condition was terminal. He had time to put his affairs in order, to settle himself that things were in place for Julie, and his last words to me were to say that he felt that he could die 'at peace with God'. The amazing grace of God at work.

Of course, no church is perfect and we have our share of disappointments and let-downs. In the best of families, conflict happens and needs to be resolved. Conflict resolution is not one of my strengths and I have had to work hard at it to overcome a tendency to react negatively. I remember, in particular, criticism made of a staff member who was young and new to the role. It needed a gentle touch and the facilitation of a healthy conversation. But out of my own defensiveness I overreacted and the situation was escalated. The outcome, owing entirely to the grace and forgiveness of all those involved, was substantially better than I deserved and we all moved forward, but certainly through no thanks to me! It is perhaps in our willingness to settle our differences that our resolve to love one another is most tested.

I think our roots laid the foundation for us to build a close community. The original planting team of the Fountain of Life shared common vision and purpose. In the early years everyone

---

68 See John 14:6.
69 This is a condition caused by exposure to asbestos dust.

was needed to turn the community centre into Sunday church and the building project required all hands on deck. There had been opposition to the work, which fuels unity and prayer. Once safely ensconced in our new worship centre, the challenge was to retain the closeness of these relationships and, as we began to grow, to see others included in this close-knit family.

We worked hard at developing the culture of family. From 2005, one of the changes we made to the way we met together on a Sunday was to incorporate our time of refreshments as part of our worship event rather than positioned at either the beginning or the end. On most Sundays, having worshipped together for thirty to forty minutes, we would break for about fifteen minutes, giving time for drinks to be served. It gave an opportunity for us to connect with new faces and catch up with one another on family news. For us Anglicans, it served as an extended form of 'The Peace', when we are encouraged to greet one another and exchange a blessing of peace. So it was a natural point at which to extend this and encouraged real community and sharing together. At a stroke this deepened our sense of community, made our morning service less formal and created bridges of connection between us all that seemed to increase our capacity to enjoy the presence of God and receive from Him. We also regularly shared lunches together.

During these times, it was very common to see people break off their conversation and pray for one another. This lowered the threshold for personal prayer considerably from needing to 'come forward' for prayer, to receiving prayer in the context of conversation and real life. Bishop David Pytches coined the phrase, 'the meeting place is the learning place for the market place'.[70] As we grew in confidence in praying for one another in this way, our Sunday experience gave us a model that was easily

---

[70] This article first appeared in *Premier Christianity* magazine, www.premierchristianity.com/Past-Issues/2016/July-2016/The-letter-of-Debby-Wright-to-the-UK-Church (accessed 25th January 2021).

transported out of the church into the home, school, place of work or whatever setting in which we found ourselves.

Another area in which our growth as 'family' developed was through our internship programme. During our time of preparation for leadership, Pippa and I had attended a week-long school of leadership run by HTB. During this, Pippa noticed that many of the activities and excellent hospitality we were witnessing relied upon the time and commitment of young adults who were serving the church on an internship programme. Could we do this back home?

A potentially major issue of accommodation had a ready solution. Pippa and I owned our own home but, at the time of succeeding Martin as leader, alternative housing for us would be provided by the diocese. So we sold the house we were living in at Saham Toney and bought a property in Ashill which we made freely available to the church for use as an interns' house.

The trustees gave the go-ahead and in the summer of 2005 we began the recruitment process for an intake in the autumn, as we planned for the internship to begin at the start of the forthcoming academic year. We were thrilled when four young people from the Fountain of Life were recruited for that very first year. The following year we had four more and in total over the past fourteen years we have seen twenty-two young adults, drawn locally and from further afield across the UK and overseas, come through our internship programme. The aim of the internship was to give each young person experience of all aspects of local church life with the opportunity to particularly focus on those areas in which they are particularly interested or gifted. It gave an opportunity for them to be involved in areas of ministry outside of their previous experience and, perhaps, would not have naturally chosen, as well as pursuing the ones where they felt more naturally competent and able.

We wanted to invest in some theological education to give the interns some teaching structure to their year. Initially we followed materials from the Vineyard Bible Institute,[71] which echoed our values and vision, and we allocated a teaching day for this once a week during term-time. Alongside this they attended various training days which we were organising for churches in the local area on such topics as leadership, prayer ministry, listening, evangelism, understanding call and vocation.

One additional feature of the year was an overseas mission. Our youth worker, Martin, and his wife, Wendy, organised the very first one. Martin is never one to do things by halves! Our first internship mission was to a group of 100-plus churches in the north-western part of India. We were invited to go back the following year and this time Martin was asked to bring his vicar along too. It was at this point that the somewhat perilous nature of the trip became apparent to me. The location was an eight-hour road trip by Land Rover from Delhi. The accommodation had no running water, it lacked basic sanitation and we were welcomed by guards armed with machine guns! By the grace of God we all survived, and chalked it up to experience.

The following year we took the team to Uganda, first to Kampala, delivering Alpha training to church leaders, and then on to Masindi Kitara diocese at the invitation of the local bishop, which gave the interns a wide range of experience of the churches and ministries. Such experiences develop faith and bond relationships in many deep ways, far beyond what would otherwise be achieved.

Our internship year proved to be such a valuable and rich teaching and training experience. So much so that in due course we needed to establish an Internship Year 2 scheme. Over the course of the years, four of our interns have graduated to become staff members.

The internship year transitioned into the New Wine Discipleship Year,[72] which added value to the teaching and

[71] Now known as Vineyard Institute, vineyardinstitute.org (accessed 1st February 2021).

[72] www.new-wine.org/discipleship-year (accessed 23rd March 2021).

training elements while retaining the values upon which our internship has been built. You will find some comments from those who have successfully completed our internship in Appendix Three.

The internship had at least two unexpected knock-on effects upon the life of the church. First, it increased at a stroke the number of young adults in the congregation. Most young adults are not islands. Each of our interns had an entourage and their friends would come and visit, or stay with them, and some became part of the church. This created a 'young adults' culture which was then attractive and helpful in gathering more local young adults. All of this helped develop a culture that was joinable for young adults and young families, which in turn is all part of the church living up to its billing as 'family'. So, in a small way, we were reaching this significant generation which is so often missing from the rural church.

One of the things that we hadn't quite foreseen was the way in which this created the opportunity for young people to meet, date and form relationships that led to marriage. This wasn't, nor should it be, of course, the goal of the internship! But, as an aside, if we believe that marriage and family is the bedrock of our society, then we need to create spaces in which young, single Christians can meet others who share their faith.

The second unexpected outcome was a greater empowering of our young people to be released into their gifts and ministries. Our older youth group especially found themselves having opportunities to serve alongside our interns, and this accelerated their growth in discipleship and mission.

For most of us, connecting Sunday to the rest of the week is a challenge. Making bridges for us to be able to transport our faith into our Monday to Saturday settings is so important for a congregation that describes itself as missionary. We are only a missionary congregation if we are a congregation of missionaries. This affects every aspect of what we include in our times of worship on a Sunday: we need preaching that will be applicable to our daily lives; we need testimonies of how other people 'like us' have experienced their faith and God in the warp and weft of life; we need to hear stories that encourage us to stand firm. We encouraged the sharing of testimony and would regularly interview members of the church, finding out what they got up to outside church, how they integrated their faith into this context and their needs for prayer. We would pray for them, and at the same time invite others facing a similar situation or context to receive prayer. It all helped to narrow the divide between sacred and secular and express our commitment to whole-life discipleship.

Jesus often conducted His conversations and acts of compassion within the context of eating together. So, we placed a high value on hospitality and felt it was important for us to attempt to model it as leaders. Usually by the end of a given week Pippa had lost count of the number fed! We would try to do as much gathering over a meal as possible, and in the early years of our leadership, we would aim to see the whole church through our doors for a meal at least once a year. Over time this became unrealistic owing to growth in numbers, and we had to change our approach. But even so, we would still host supper parties with people chosen at random which mixed people up and created some interesting and dynamic gatherings.

We held Newcomers Suppers regularly, which gave opportunities for new people to meet some of the team, hear something of the history and vision of the church, and begin to find their place of belonging.

Home groups are the pastoral glue in the church. As a church grows it is impossible for the leader to pastor everyone. Shortly after the exodus from Egypt and the dramatic crossing of the Red Sea, Moses was left with the challenge of pastoring the Israelites – a challenge that he initially attempted to face alone. When his father-in-law, Jethro, came visiting, he rebuked Moses for trying to meet all the needs of the people without recourse to others. 'What you are doing is not good,' he said, and suggested that Moses adopt a different approach, encouraging leaders to be appointed of smaller groups to deal with the everyday cases, leaving Moses the time and space to handle the more complex (Exodus 18:13-26). Wisdom indeed. Likewise, we have operated a delegated model of pastoral care within the church. It spreads responsibility, releases gifts and makes the task of leadership for the overall leader more holistic and mission-focused.

These groups worship together, engage in Bible study, minister to and pray for one another, drink coffee and eat cake. Many do more together: barbecues, outings, even holidays together. They are the lifeblood of the church. We appoint the leaders and trust them to hear from God for themselves as to how the groups should function, but they are all expected to be places of accountability, support and nurture. We recommend a balance of worship, prayer and Bible study, but leave it to the individual groups to decide the nature of that balance and themes. I recommend meeting weekly during term-time, but leave it to the groups and their leaders to decide on frequency. Groups are dynamic, and healthy groups change shape and multiply, but they are the first line of our pastoral care provision.

Pippa and I gathered the leaders of the groups together three times each year to eat together and find out how the life of each group was faring. This created a strong accountability structure – vital to ensure effective delegation – and kept me as the overall leader in touch with the pastoral life of the church.

We have also encouraged the growth of Life groups. A Life group is an accountability group. It is formed when two or three people agree to meet together to pray and share life. It is intended to be a safe place of transparency within the intimacy of sharing with just one or two others. These groups are an informal part of our life together and deliver at another discipleship level. I have noticed how many have adopted a 'disciple-making culture': entering into the importance of being discipled by someone who has something to teach us and then discipling someone who is learning from us. We don't formally register or measure them. Anecdotally we know that they are increasing in number, but we leave it to individuals to take the initiative. It is also another way in which we have the building blocks in place that cultivate the value of family and belonging.

The gift of 'helps' is tucked away in Paul's lists (1 Corinthians 12:28, KJV), and is sometimes overlooked in our consideration of the Spirit's gifts, but it is not to be underestimated in its power or effect. Think of the four men who carry their paralysed friend and set him before Jesus (Mark 2:1-12); those who were instructed to give food to the daughter of Jairus – after the miracle of being raised from the dead, it would have been unfortunate for her to die of malnutrition (Luke 8:53-56); Stephen, waiting on tables (Acts 6:1-6); or Timothy, Epaphroditus, Priscilla and Aquila all helping Paul in practical ways (see for example Philippians 2:25).

Adam and Julia had been members of the church since they got married thirteen years before. Now with two children, Julia was a teacher and Adam a forensic scientist. Adam also volunteered at his children's primary school when he could. On one particular day in November 2018 he was on his way home with a car full of gardening equipment when he was involved in a serious road traffic accident. He doesn't fully remember what happened, but he was airlifted to a specialist hospital with traumatic head injuries. A couple of weeks beforehand in their home group during prayer, a prophetic picture had been shared. In this picture, Adam and Julia were in the fiery furnace with Daniel's three friends. Just like those three men, they were not burnt and nor did they smell of smoke. They were totally unharmed. The word given to Adam and Julia was, 'God is with you in the furnace.'[73]

So, when a policeman arrived at Julia's school to break the news, even before he spoke, Julia's immediate thought was, 'This could be the fiery furnace, but it will be OK in the end.' She received an overwhelming sense of peace, but it was

---

[73] See Daniel 3 for the context of this story and verse 25 in particular. The person sharing the picture was reminded of this verse when praying for Adam and Julia in the group and interpreted it as God's promise to them.

receiving the gift of 'helps' that sustained her through the ensuing period. Julia and her two young children needed practical support and the presence of others. Immediately on receiving the news, Julia phoned her good friend Helen, who dropped everything to accompany her to the hospital and provide her with ongoing support. Under Helen's guidance, the church rallied around with meals, prayer and offers of help.

It has been a long road to recovery for Adam. There have been many times when different people have sowed in some wise words to turn away negative thoughts and give God's perspective and wisdom.

There are so many other stories that I would become aware of in which people would simply see a need and respond. Often someone would take responsibility for organising a team to provide meals for a family suffering from bereavement or illness, or step in to provide respite care for someone caring for a loved one, or provide childcare to enable a couple to have a much-needed weekend away together.

People were freely giving their time to help others move house, engage in practical projects such as painting and decorating, garden care, repairing fences, litter picking. These practices of love in action were spilling over into the wider community. Various groups developed the habit of prayer walking their communities, looking out for individuals or homes where there seemed to be particular needs for practical help.

This ministry of mercy was an area which we knew we were called to press into (Matthew 23:23). Before the advent of foodbanks, we had set up The Lord's Foodstore. Members of the church were encouraged to buy one extra food item during the week as a gift and bring it along on a Sunday morning. All the gifts were collected up and distributed to those who we knew were facing particular hardship.

In addition, each year in the spring and autumn we held a Clothes Swap. People were encouraged to bring items that were in good condition and at the same time to pick up a new outfit. In the end, this became a somewhat laborious process and wasn't the best way of meeting those in particular need of support. We also maintained a furniture store, but there was a limit on the amount of furniture we could store at any one time, and although there were times when we had just the right match for a particular need, this was a bit unpredictable and logistically difficult.

In 2006, we had heard about The Besom project and went down to visit them in south-west London. The vision of The Besom was (and still is) to be 'the bridge by which we as followers of Jesus are equipped and enthused to give what we have to those around us who are in need'.[74] In particular, it provides a bridge between those with money, time, skills or things to give and those in need. So a small team led by Pippa was established to set up a local Besom centre.

This did not develop in the way we had hoped, but there were two particular areas of ongoing fruitful ministry that continued. One was connection to a local women's refuge to which we were able to supply clothes, toiletries and sometimes furnishings to help people at such a critical and vulnerable point in their lives. The second was the provision of Christmas hampers to those in need. Members of the church were encouraged to donate basic foods and treats and a team would then wrap and pack hampers to look as well presented and special as possible – to treat those who 'have not' as royalty! These would be distributed to those we knew about who were facing particular hardship at this often challenging season and who were struggling to make ends meet. This was something that the whole church was able to embrace, and receipt of these hampers would be met with much joy and thankfulness.

The primary need, though, for many was a financial one, and one of the hallmarks of 'family' is that you do all you can to support one another in times of hardship. In a survey of our membership, we discovered that 15 per cent had been helped financially in a time of need by others. We already had in place

---

[74] www.besom.com (accessed 26th January 2021).

a Loan Fund which was available for those facing a crisis and for whom a small sum of money would make a significant difference. However, this was not easy to administer and we were aware that adding to a person's debt, even though interest-free, was not helping them resolve financial issues.

Debt is an issue that often carries with it shame and guilt as well as a sense of complete helplessness or powerlessness in finding a way forward. It can be a place full of despair, darkness and one without hope. It can be an emotive subject. I remember, about twenty years ago, preaching on the issue of money and touched on the issue of debt and was taken to task afterwards by a couple of people who, through no particular fault of their own, had found themselves in debt. I had tried to be careful in how I preached, but obviously had not been careful enough, and the reaction demonstrated the sensitivity of the subject.

Then in 2007, along came Heather. She felt called to oversee all of our 'Mercy' activities. Heather had already set up an emergency prayer chain, which was a way of us releasing people to pray for needs as they arose. This operated on the basis of texting needs through a dedicated mobile phone line. A need was texted and then circulated to all those who had volunteered to be part of the chain.

Astrid now looks after this for us and there are some fifty people who are willing to pray, and have signed a confidentiality agreement to respect the privacy of those for whom we are praying. This releases a significant amount of committed and focused prayer. It is fantastic to see the way in which prayers have been answered with healing, comfort and direction. It has been a service much called upon during Covid-19.

Heather's heart was to help us become more effective in meeting practical needs, especially financial ones. She was already running a financial services business supporting local businesses, charities and churches with bookkeeping, payroll and employment support services. Given that her working time was so immersed in the world of finance, she did have a little bit of an argument with the Lord as to why He thought it would be a good idea for her to do finance in her spare time as well! But this seemed to be the call of God and she responded in obedience and faith. Particularly after the 2008 financial crash, we became much more aware of the needs within the community and our focus shifted even further to those outside the church family.

We changed the Loan Fund into a Gift Fund and Heather became the first point of contact for this, sifting requests or recommendations and then presenting to me for approval those she felt had met the criteria. Included in Heather's consideration would be the overall financial position of the person, their ability to obtain help from other sources, the size of contribution required and all the while attempting to listen to the prompting of the Holy Spirit. Of course, it soon became apparent that the need far outstripped our capacity to give. There were limits to how much we could help. Some debt situations needed professional help to resolve. It was also apparent that, while issues of debt may arise out of unforeseen circumstances such as loss of livelihood or unexpected illness, earlier preventative intervention in money management would often have helped.

Heather was on the original steering group of Thetford Foodbank, seeded by Trussell Trust,[75] which expanded to cover some other market towns in the area. This gave us access to a more organised distribution of food to those in our community, and became the place to which the contents of The Lord's Foodstore were donated.

Heather opened up a conversation with Christians Against Poverty (CAP)[76] to explore how we might be able to work in partnership. CAP was started in 1996 by John Kirkby, who himself had faced bankruptcy but used that experience, and his

---

[75] See thetford.foodbank.org.uk and www.trusselltrust.org (accessed 26th January 2021).
[76] capuk.org (accessed 26th January 2021).

expertise within the finance industry, to work with those with this need and set them free from the crippling effects of debt. In 2010 we began to run The CAP Money Course,[77] a three-session course establishing principles of budgeting and money management. The material was excellent, but encouraging people to attend was rather more difficult. This was not just an issue that we faced locally, but was an experience replicated nationwide. Most people who were not facing issues of debt felt that they were managing their money perfectly fine and did not need any help. We were not connecting with those who had the greatest need, for various reasons. The shame, stigma, guilt and fear that so often accompany debt did not help, of course.

Many of those who did complete the course and applied the principles found that they moved from seemingly not having enough money to having excess to save, give or spend. The course did not offer a solution to those already facing serious issues of debt, and Heather wanted us to be able to do more. After further conversations with CAP, the 'more' became an invitation to set up a debt centre.

CAP debt centres are run through the local church working in partnership with others. One of the values held dear by CAP is to establish the link with the local church, show God's love and bring people into God's kingdom. It enabled us to provide support to people locally, but also to tap into the excellent debt management services available from CAP's professionally trained staff based at the centre in Bradford.

However, establishing a centre required a significant investment of time and money. First, it needed a manager. Very conveniently, God had added to our number John, who had been doing this work before in Exmouth. He was prepared to do the job on a voluntary basis, which was an enormous help in enabling us to make a start. Second, it needed finance.

[77] The CAP Money Course is a money management course developed by Christians Against Poverty that teaches people budgetary skills. See www.capmoney.org (accessed 2nd March 2021).

Donations from individuals, a grant from Cinnamon Network[78] and a contribution from the Fountain of Life enabled us to step out on the journey, and the mid-Norfolk CAP debt centre was established in April 2013. The Fountain of Life agreed to underwrite the costs on the basis that other churches in the area would be contacted and sources of funding explored. One church in Dereham, under the leadership of Jon,[79] stepped up to be alongside us financially.[80]

Most CAP debt centres are based in cities or towns. We were positioned in the middle of nowhere serving a wide geographic area. This meant that our manager John often had to travel up to an hour to visit clients and build up a team of befrienders from other churches more local to where the clients were based.

A management group was established to oversee the work attended by representatives from five local churches. John did an amazing job in establishing the centre, and in 2014 he moved to run the Norwich debt centre. At this point Heather felt that the Lord was calling her to take on the debt centre leadership. Initially she gave her time voluntarily and was even prepared for her business to employ someone to take on some of her clients, to release her time. In due course we were able to employ Heather for sixteen hours per week, although there continued to be seasons when Heather prioritised the debt centre over her own livelihood.

Over the seven years since it has been established, twenty-four new households each year have been helped through this centre. Each household can be with us for up to four years plus. The running costs of our centre are £11,000 per annum, but thus far these continue to be met by the faithful giving of individuals and grants obtained from elsewhere.

---

[78] www.cinnamonnetwork.co.uk (accessed 8th March 2021).

[79] Jon is the pastor of the Wellspring Family Church, Dereham, see www.wellspringfamilychurch.org (accessed 25th March 2021).

[80] We were thrilled when in September 2019 Dereham Baptist Church agreed with CAP to start a new debt centre in the town. See www.derehambaptist.org (accessed 25th March 2021).

There are many stories of people who have been transformed through the connection we have made with them through CAP.

Doris[81] was someone who, when Heather first encountered her, was living in isolation, and though she was still working, she had serious financial issues owing to an addiction. Heather spent time praying with her and talking with her about her isolation and the need to get out. She offered her a befriender, but also invited her to church. Doris completed the Alpha course, came to faith and joined the church. She is now about to go debt-free and has a network of supportive friends in a family.

Rose was declared to be debt-free while attending an Alpha course with us. This is how she describes its impact on her life:

> When I first got in contact with Heather and CAP I was worrying all the time about money. Now I'm debt-free and I feel like a new person. I can't believe what a difference it's made to my life. I now go to church and have an amazing circle of friends.

Keira made contact. She was physically and mentally disabled, with failing eyesight. She was in a dire situation, living in a first-floor flat which was not at all clean. Heather recruited the involvement of other agencies, signed her up to CAP, and protected her from loan sharks and other predators who were taking advantage of her vulnerability. She was rehoused, attended a CAP client evangelistic event where she was completely overwhelmed by the Holy Spirit, invited Jesus to be her Lord and Saviour, joined a local church and was baptised the following year with Heather in supportive attendance.

One of the worst living conditions encountered by Heather was that of Dominic, who was in significant debt owing to having taken on more commitments than his income allowed.

---

[81] While we have permission to tell these stories, all the names of CAP clients have been changed to preserve anonymity.

He was on minimum wage, with limited hours as a cleaner. His work was fifteen miles away, which required him to finance a car which he was unable to afford. We connected him to a local church that helped him clear the house and redecorate. We sorted out the provision of an alternative car, which enabled him to continue to work. He is now living debt-free.

In 2015, Heather received CAP's national award of CAP Money Coordinator of the Year in recognition of her outstanding work in making the work of CAP Money known to churches in our region. Heather is a champion for CAP in the area, and as one of its trained speakers is often out and about carrying the flag of CAP and the needs of the poor to other churches.

The following year, Heather came across the work of Acts 435,[82] an initiative that allows people to give money directly to others. It operates on the basis of a website which features needs that have been monitored and assessed by advocates from local churches. So all the needs presented have been verified as authentic and real. The need, once posted on the website, is broadcast anonymously and those wanting to give can access the website and give equally anonymously. Our part as a local church would be to provide the advocate, who would be the go-between for the person with the need and it being posted on the website. Their role would be to visit and verify those coming forward with needs. We made this need for an advocate known to the church, and Trevor responded. Trevor and his wife, Ruth, are extraordinarily compassionate people who already had busy and demanding roles as foster parents. But Trevor felt called to do this, and that makes all the difference.

Thinking back to The Besom, Acts 435 is our way today of matching those who are able to give with those in need, and is proving a very effective way of achieving this in a rural area such as ours.

---

[82] acts435.org.uk (accessed 26th January 2021).

Finally in this chapter, as a family we have known our fair share of tragedies, losses, family breakdowns, untimely deaths and disappointments. Times when our chief response is simply to mourn alongside those who are grieving or suffering. In our experience, these are the times of greatest privilege and opportunity to show the compassion of Christ and to point to our greatest hope in the promise of resurrection and new life.

The very first funeral I took as senior leader of the Fountain was that of Tim, a young man in our church aged just seventeen, who was killed in a car accident. It happened in an instant and there was no time for the family to say goodbye. Attending the funeral of your child is perhaps every parent's worst nightmare. I remember the funeral service well. Tim was a popular young man and that day the church was full of his young friends coming to terms with what had happened. Despite the enormity of the loss, it was a faith-filled time together, with two of Tim's closest friends and his two brothers contributing in poems, shared memories and experiences. I really can't remember what I spoke about, although it seemed to give hope and comfort at the time. Tim had grown up through our children's and youth programme so it was an opportunity for me to talk about faith and give people the opportunity to choose Jesus. It was, though, the faith and confidence of his family, especially his parents and brothers, that spoke so much more powerfully. In the midst of grief there was such a sense of steadfast, confident hope in the promise of resurrection and new life.

Enid was one of the first people we met on arrival in Norfolk, and she soon became one of our dearest friends. One day on her way over to the Fountain to pray, her car skidded on ice and she was instantly killed. We were just about to go to Uganda on mission with the interns and I remember that on hearing the news I pummelled my study door with my fists. Not perhaps the most godly of reactions, but it helped me express my sorrow and, if I'm honest, anger (with God) that this should have happened. Once again her funeral service was turned into a time of thanksgiving for her life and was filled with joy and faith. It was another opportunity to present the gospel and invite a response. We looked at the story of the raising of Lazarus and applied to Enid the question that some asked on the death of Lazarus: 'Could not he who opened the eyes of the blind man have kept this man from dying?' (John 11:37). Facing and coming up with some answers to that question had helped me in my own grief, and I think it helped others too.

Shaun was the son of Wendy, who married Martin when Shaun was fourteen. Martin loved Shaun as if he were his own. Shaun too had come through our youth group during Martin's leadership. As a young man he was well liked and sociable; he loved sport and was a keen footballer. He cared for others and was described as 'loving the unloved'. But, as many do, he had difficulties loving and fully accepting himself. This led to an ongoing problem with addiction to alcohol and other substances. Despite lots of people praying and loads of support from his family, the day came when Shaun decided to take his own life.

Nothing can quite prepare you for an event like this. The natural response for those of us who knew and loved him was to question whether there was more that we could have done. In cases like this, feelings of guilt, recrimination, shame as well as anger can all mingle with the sense of devastating loss, and especially so for those closest to the person. It was the same for those most closely connected to Shaun. In his Bible, though, Shaun had underlined Ezekiel 36:26: 'I will give you a new heart and put a new spirit in you.' He may have had difficulty in appropriating this verse in this life, but it gave us all the encouragement we needed to hold on to hope.

Often, all we can do is walk with those who are wrestling with grief and loss – walking at their pace, not ours. It's yet another opportunity for the family of God to come together in love. I have come to value times of loss and suffering as the crucible in which our faith is honed and shaped, and as opportunities for bonds to be forged between us that time will never break. For it is undoubtedly true that a community that authentically demonstrates the love of God will grow. Our society craves it, individuals need it, and the Trinity of God is totally committed to reproducing it. Love has to be the hallmark of Spirit-filled community and it helps produce a family that grows.

5

Reaching a New Generation

Start children off on the way they should go,
and even when they are old they will not turn from it.
(Proverbs 22:6)

Reaching children and young people with the gospel is essential in passing on the baton of faith to the next generation. Surveys consistently show that around two-thirds of practising Christians come to faith before the age of eighteen and around 40 per cent before the age of twelve.[83] In our work with children and young people, our vision is for there to be a golden thread of continuity from one age group to the next. As children grow older, we always need to be planning for the next stage of their development, having age-related activities and groups to which they can belong. However excellent our work with children in one age group may be, we will lose them if we don't intentionally plan for the next stage of their discipleship. Often it is the critical teenage years where we are most at risk of seeing fallout. We will still lose some, but let us aim to 'bear … fruit that will last' (John 15:16).

One way or another, we have always sought to protect this 'golden thread' with provision for children across the years. On

---

[83] ministry-to-children.com/childrens-ministry-statistics/#childhood (accessed 11th March 2020).

Sundays, we have '1 Kings' for children from Reception through to Year 2, '2 Kings' for children from Year 3 through to Year 5; 'Genesis' for Year 6 through to Year 9 and 'Beatitudes' for Years 10-13.[84]

We have agreed outcomes for each age group. For example, we hope that by the time of completing 2 Kings (by the age of ten) children will:

- Know Jesus as their friend.
- Know their way around the Bible: the difference between Old and New Testaments, number of books, different types of literature and so forth.
- Have the foundation of Scripture laid in their lives through story, memory verses and encouragement to read the Bible at home.
- Be introduced to the healing ministry and grow accustomed to ministering to each other in the power of the Holy Spirit, becoming comfortable with the use of spiritual gifts such as the prophetic.
- Be introduced to different models of prayer.
- Be given an opportunity to experience worship as a group.

This is then built upon as young people navigate through our youth groups to increase their doctrinal understanding, their ability to interpret the Scriptures, their confidence in who they are in Christ, their ability to share testimony and exercise the gifts of the Spirit, and explore calling and vision.

Youngsters need role models, and one of our mantras has been that every age group would disciple the one below and be discipled by the one above. Children need to see what it looks like to be a Christian teenager, teenagers need young adults to show that it is possible to be a Christian beyond childhood,

---

[84] During Covid-19 we have been running online Sunday Kids Church and youth hangout meetings.

single young adults need healthy families who will look out for them, young marrieds need the support and care of older couples, parents value the support and guidance of those who have been through the stages of life, older people can model how to finish well and pass on their wisdom, encouragement and strength through the generations. At the same time they sometimes need practical support and companionship on the journey, which younger people in the family of God can provide.

We have always been blessed with a highly committed and gifted team of volunteers who sacrificially give of their time and energy to work with our children and young people. It is vital work. It is a work that calls for perseverance.

I remember the following story, set during the First World War. One soldier, mortally wounded from an artillery shell, was being comforted by another who asked if there was anything he could do for him. 'Yes,' replied the dying soldier. 'Please go to this address and tell him that what he taught me when I was young has helped me to die in this place.'

Many months later the surviving soldier made it safely home and duly went to the address and gave the message to the man who opened the door. 'May God forgive me,' came the response, 'for I gave up teaching Sunday school because I felt that I was not making any difference.'[85] Never underestimate the power of the seed of the gospel to produce life.

Teams need leaders. As mentioned earlier, Martin Spaul was our first paid youth worker. He and his wife, Wendy, laid the foundations for our youth work. They built a culture of family, influenced by the wisdom of 'belong, believe, behave'. This is the understanding that our core beliefs are often shaped by those closest to us and that, in turn, our way of behaving is then influenced by these beliefs and values. We love people into behaving. Martin and Wendy put this into practice. They poured

---

[85] I cannot find a written reference to this story, but have told it verbatim according to my memory.

their hearts into the young people and it bore fruit. The young people grew in their relationship with God, with one another and in confidence. The youth group adopted Alpha and began to lead groups around the local area – at one stage four Youth Alpha courses were being held simultaneously. Discipleship groups were introduced to help build close relationships between the young people and to enable Bible study, prayer and worship. Martin and Wendy hosted lots of informal gatherings at their home with games, adventures, barbecues, day trips, residential camping activities and the obligatory annual pilgrimage to Soul Survivor. They increasingly organised the young people to engage in evangelistic activities, including door-to-door missions, practical action in the community, street theatre and much else.

After serving as youth worker for ten years, in 2008 Martin felt that it was the right time for him to step down. He already had his eye on his successor. He had been mentoring one of our interns, Adam Jackson, and recommended that we appoint him to the post. At the same time we also wanted to create a new post of families and children's worker to help support our church families and those on the fringes. This was a significant step for the church to take. It was one thing to employ a youth worker but quite another to have a children and families worker. This was breaking new ground, and we were not quite sure about the shape of the role.

As we were considering this, a member of our church, Andrea, approached me outlining a vision she felt God had given her to see a 'families centre' established. She could not see completely how it would work itself out, but she knew the first step. Like the boy with 'five small barley loaves and two small fish', she could give what she had in her hand (John 6:9). She had many years' experience of leading a preschool and believed that the first step towards her vision was to establish a Christian preschool operating under the authority of the Fountain of Life. She was not quite sure how this fitted with the families worker post but felt that she should apply – and I was sure that she was

God's choice. Both this appointment and that of the youth worker were put on the agenda to be discussed at our forthcoming annual trustees' vision day.

The day before this meeting we were visited by someone with experience and a reputation in prophetic ministry. She met the staff team and then later prayed for Pippa and me. As she prayed for us, she sensed the Holy Spirit saying that there was a shockwave coming. Not everyone would understand it, but there would be a release of energy, of power, like a bolt of lightning hitting. We would be appointing people into staff positions who were not the most likely candidates. God was raising people up into position, and people would be amazed at those who were coming into the foreground.

The following day it was unanimously agreed to move forward with the appointment of both Adam and Andrea. As you can imagine, the trustees were then very heartened and reassured to learn that a prophet[86] had gone ahead of them. It's also a good example of how the prophetic can come alongside the church leader to affirm direction and the decisions taken.

So, Andrea pioneered First Steps preschool. We formed its own management group with delegated powers from the board of trustees. We gave some 'seed money' to help establish it, but it is not financed by the church in an ongoing way. Like any other preschool, it relies upon fees from parents and the statutory state provision, and is subject to the external assessment of OFSTED, whose findings have consistently ranged from Good to Outstanding. It is staffed by seven excellent practitioners who share a Christian faith, and in 2019 there were twenty-eight children who attended.

Andrea has built an excellent relationship with the local Church of England primary school, and our preschool has established a reputation for excellence in the local area. She

---

[86] While all in the body of Christ are encouraged to exercise the prophetic gift (1 Corinthians 14:1), some are used by God more regularly in the ministry and office of a prophet (Ephesians 4:11).

considered First Steps to be a family within a family. Andrea placed a high value in connecting with and supporting the whole family surrounding the child. The family of any new child received a home visit, and Andrea worked hard to establish strong relationships with each of them.

First Steps built upon the work of Noah's Ark, a long-standing weekly parent and toddlers group, which has been part of the journey of faith for many and another anchor point in connecting people into the church. Andrea also introduced Family Fun times. These are opportunities to gather families and mark the key Christian festivals such as Christmas and Easter. At Halloween she organised an alternative Light Party, which was always welcomed by parents in the community as well as the church, being seen as a safe place for their children.

Who Let the Dads Out is another initiative that Andrea established – an occasional Saturday morning enabling men to spend time with their children over brunch and activities. It helped us build relationships with men and has been another access point for those outside the church.

It's worth recognising that Andrea's original vision to see a family centre established has not yet been fully realised – at least, not in the way that she first envisaged. But the journey would never have begun without that initial 'big' vision. It encouraged a step to be taken, a few more steps have been added and we value all that God has done on the journey so far.

Meanwhile, our new youth worker was also settling into his post. Looking back on this time, Adam Jackson comments:

> My transition to becoming youth pastor and media guy [we had added media responsibilities to Adam's brief in view of his competency in this area] was significant as I had an inkling that it would happen but it never seemed possible. It was a real affirmation of calling to be asked to take over from Martin.

He ran discipleship groups for the young people as well as a monthly outreach event and, together with his wife, Shona, organised separate weekends away for the boys and girls.[87]

Adam's strength, similar to his predecessor, lay in building strong relationships with the young people. He was inspired about the importance of mentoring young people and regularly went for walks individually with the youngsters, talking about life and God. Even though these young people are now in their twenties, many of them are still in close contact with Adam.

Since Adam's appointment to St Stephen's,[88] we have tended to employ two or more part-time youth workers, rather than relying on one full-time post, enabling us to minister more effectively to the diverse needs of young people across the age range of eleven to eighteen. It brings with it all of the benefits that come with diversity of strengths, passions and gifting, which far outweigh any tensions that can be caused by different ways of doing things. Three years ago our original youth worker, Martin, came back on staff as our lead youth worker to help bring cohesion and direction to the team. He remembers being prayed with by a member of Heidi Baker's team from Iris Ministries[89] and given the word, 'You're a bus driver.' As he reflected upon this, he thought how it's the leader's job to tell people the destination and get everyone on the bus.

There are so many threads to our work with children and young people. There is not enough space to cover it all. Activities come and go, group names change, new ideas are tested, but certain principles remain.

Youth work is rooted in relationship. Usually it requires at least one paid youth worker who can be set aside to invest the level of time commitment required to nurture the growth and development of a team. Effective youth work may need a paid leader, but it also relies upon those who have a vision for

---

[87] This would prove to be the birthing of the Intents event referred to earlier.

[88] Referred to in Chapter 3.

[89] www.irisglobal.org (accessed 26th January 2021).

working with young people and who will freely give of their time. It always needs a team of dedicated people who are passionate about their relationship with God and love young people. We call them 'volunteers', but this fails to adequately describe the huge commitment week by week that so many make in helping us to meet the needs of our young people.

It also needs a church that is willing to invest long term in children's and youth work and a leadership prepared to provide accountability and support. More than this, though, it needs the whole church to embrace young people, to show an interest in them individually, to encourage and support them and to provide a culture that helps them to know they are valued not just by God, but also by the generations that have gone before them.

Real discipleship is conducted through the journey of shared lives. Perhaps our greatest contribution is living our lives in such a way that gives our young people a model that encourages them to trust God for themselves and be inspired to follow Him. It's a contribution made by each member of our team, past and present.

The children and young people who are in our church on a Sunday morning are usually the ones who are in Christian families. As a missionary congregation, we are called to prioritise engaging with unchurched children and young people. This is, by and large, a disempowered group – they don't get to choose to come to church. They rely on parents or other adults taking them to places, and if Sunday morning church is not on the family calendar, then it's hard for them to come to us – especially primary school-aged children. How do we reach them?

Kidz Klub was an answer to this question – church for unchurched children on a Saturday morning.

Tim, a member of our church, first heard about Kidz Klub at the Children's Ministry conference in Eastbourne in January 2001. Kidz Klub, a monthly club for children, supported by home visiting, began in New York under the leadership of Bill

Wilson at Metro Ministries, New York,[90] and was introduced to the UK by Frontline Church in Liverpool.[91] For the previous seven years we had been running an annual holiday club during the summer for children aged five to eleven and wanted to build on this. Kidz Klub looked as if it could be the answer to this desire. So, in December of 2001, three of us visited Frontline, including Tim. He had come to faith eight years previously one Sunday morning at St Nicholas'. God gave him a heart for church children almost immediately after coming to faith but, during our visit, God put a burden on his heart for reaching unchurched children with the gospel. He caught a vision for introducing Kidz Klub at the Fountain and felt God was challenging him to reduce his paid work in order to free up a day a week. Tim at that stage was project manager for a building construction company, but approached his employers who agreed to release him from October 2002. Tim took a salary cut and Kidz Klub in mid-Norfolk was born. He recruited a team and on 18th January 2003 our first monthly Klub was held with fifty-six children attending. Thereafter, once a month, children gathered for a Saturday morning with an opportunity to hear the gospel. Here are Tim's reflections on this time:

> We saw a need for a place where kids could learn about God and His Son Jesus throughout the year, not just in the summer. Thankfully, God asked me to help Him put this in place so that's how our first Kidz Klub started; a fast-moving, fun-packed Saturday morning with a Christian message. The Bible tells us how God just loves spending time with kids, seeing them have fun, teaching them and watching them grow. All who are involved with Kidz Klub share His passion. Joining in God's vision for

[90] This is now known as Metro World Child, see www.metroworldchild.org (accessed 26th January 2021).
[91] www.frontline.org.uk (accessed 26th January 2021).

kids in Norfolk is great fun, at times challenging but always rewarding.

The vision of Kidz Klub is quite simple: to give every child the opportunity to choose Jesus. There are songs, panto and games before exploring the theme of the day, supported by craft, refreshments, games and, of course, prizes. The monthly Klub is then supported by a home-visiting programme which helps the children apply what they learn and us to connect with the whole family.

In 2005, Maryanne, from a nearby church, came to see me. She had a vision to start up a new Kidz Klub a few miles north of Ashill. Maryanne, who had previous experience as a schools worker with mid-Norfolk Youth for Christ, had a vision not only for the monthly Klub but also for building relationships with schools. She was also involved in running a Churches Together holiday club in her local market town and wanted to bring this under the umbrella of Kidz Klub so that a monthly Klub could start in her community. It was a similar starting point to the way our existing Klub had originated. She came with some personal financial support which would be transferred to Kidz Klub, and in September 2006 we welcomed Maryanne on to our staff team. This multiplied our monthly Klubs, holiday clubs and connections with families, and initiated our schools ministry.

Tim and Maryanne worked together in further developing Kidz Klub for six years, at which point Tim sensed it was the right time to pass on his responsibilities and identified Matt Beckett as his successor. Matt had come to faith at the Fountain and served as an intern with us following his time at university, where he completed a degree in drama. After his internship, Matt was initially appointed to work alongside Adam as youth worker. In due time he felt more of a calling towards Kidz Klub and families work. Matt was a natural choice to succeed Tim, taking responsibility for Kidz Klub in Ashill and developing relationships with schools in the local area. We were invited to take on responsibility for Open the Book,[92] a project in our local village school which had been initiated through the parish church. It offers primary school children an opportunity to hear key Bible stories from a team of Christians from local churches who present the stories during assemblies. Matt established a team of volunteers to do this. Running this project has further built on the excellent relationships established with the school by our preschool and ongoing Kidz Klub involvement. Tim has not lost his passion for Kidz Klub, regularly serving on team and overseeing the ministry as one of our church trustees.

As far as possible, we have sought to develop staff in line with the Spirit's leading and calling within them and allowed that to a certain extent to shape the detail of our focus and priorities. Matt is an illustration of this. His job has evolved during his time here, shaped by particular areas that God has put on his heart. From being involved in Kidz Klub he developed a growing sense of the home as being the primary place of discipleship and the need to equip parents in sharing faith. So we expanded his role to include space for this to be developed.

Under Tim, Maryanne and Matt's leadership, Kidz Klub has grown to around 300 children regularly attending the monthly Klubs or being home-visited. More than twenty schools have welcomed our teams to deliver assemblies, lunchtime clubs and RE days, homework clubs and events such as Christmas and Easter Experience, which help children to understand the true meaning behind these festivals.

But the team always consider that our core ministry is the two monthly Klubs supported by home-visiting and the discipling work that goes on alongside.

Kidz Klub has also seen the growth of what we call 'young team'. When children reached the age of eleven, which is at the top end of the Kidz Klub age range, we found that they still

---

92 Open the Book is a national project resourced by the Bible Society, see www.biblesociety.org.uk/get-involved/open-the-book/ (accessed 23rd March 2021).

wanted to be involved. So we developed 'young team' to keep them connected, engaged and discipled. At the same time, discipleship groups were formed to meet midweek which enabled some of these young people to be integrated with those who came along to the Fountain of Life on a Sunday morning. These groups, hosted by volunteers in their homes, are safe places for youngsters to gather with food, fun and Bible study. It's a place where they have the freedom to talk about issues and concerns, pray for one another and be loved. This is our primary way of keeping a discipleship relationship with our young people. We estimate that around forty to fifty of our young people have been discipled in the church through the Kidz Klub route.

Two stories illustrate this. Connor came along to Kidz Klub and loved it so much that he joined the young team. He also joined a discipleship group and made a commitment to Jesus. His next step was to be baptised, and he continued to make Kidz Klub his spiritual home as he grew in his faith. He became increasingly interested in the technical side, and by the time he left Kidz Klub to go to university, he had become our go-to man for all matters connected to sound or visuals for this particular Kidz Klub. No surprise, then, that he went to university to study theatre management.

Ellie had been coming to Kidz Klub since she was aged eight and again loved it so much that she transitioned into young team and discipleship group. Nine years after first coming to Kidz Klub, she was baptised. She preached at Focus, our evening service led by young people, and her clarity, confidence and content were impressive, along with the evident integrity of her faith being lived out in her home and college. She and her mum, Julie, came to a missional community connected to Kidz Klub[93] and transitioned to our Sunday gatherings.

---

[93] Called Refresh, this activity is described in Chapter 7.

Kidz Klub has been so significant in enabling us to reach unchurched children and their families – indeed, a book could probably be written about its story alone!

Our involvement with schools led to other opportunities emerging. Maryanne initiated taking CAP Money into schools, teaching children how to budget and handle money well. She became increasingly aware of the need for early intervention for children who were at risk of exclusion. At the time, Norfolk had the highest rate of children excluded at primary school level nationwide. Through her research she learned of an organisation working in this field called Transforming Lives for Good (TLG)[94] and wanted to make its programmes available to some of our local schools. She volunteered to organise this locally and, at the beginning of 2019, we partnered with TLG to provide mentoring support and early intervention for those in our local primary and junior schools most at risk of exclusion. This is a challenge for us. It requires a team of people who are willing to commit one hour each week during term-time to one child. It also requires us to find the money to pay for the resources, training and support that we receive from TLG. This is a new venture for us, stretching our resources once again, and its sustainability has yet to be proven.

Determining whether or not we respond to initiatives and ideas like this is the task of leaders. We have to sift the good ideas from the God ones, and I can't claim infallibility in my discernment. It may be unwise for us to keep saying 'yes' to these invitations. We do always need to be assessing our priorities in relation to the strength we have. There are times when we have overreached ourselves and had to pull back. But, while trying to exercise some pastoral wisdom about it, I would rather stretch until the risk of breaking point is reached than stay within the confines of what we know to be safe.

Youth Café is another answer to the way we connect with children and young people outside the church – this time

---

[94] www.tlg.org.uk (accessed 26th January 2021).

particularly reaching out to older young people. Matt Schwarzenberger had come to us from Holy Trinity Leicester as an intern. After the internship finished, a position within Kidz Klub became available and Matt was appointed. In due time he felt called more to older young people, and we moved him to be one of our youth workers. He pioneered a café church for young people on a Sunday morning, meeting at a well-known coffee house in a nearby market town. We had previously started an after-school youth café on a local estate and later also in the village of Ashill, when the local youth club closed. However, attendance at the Ashill drop-in began to decline and it became a drain on resources to keep it going. We brought it to a close and this released time and energy to focus on the new project. This gave our own young people a mission activity to engage in, a place to invite their friends and an opportunity to make contact with young people outside the church, who were more familiar with the surroundings of the coffee house than our church. It's a work that we lead in partnership with other churches. This had grown to a regular attendance of more than thirty before Covid-19.

Integrating young people from outside the church also highlighted to Matt a need to change the way in which we discipled our young people. Up to this point, young people from our children's programme transitioned to youth around the age of movement from primary to secondary education. This meant that we were moving children on at the time they were already facing a significant change to their schooling and friendship circle. Matt proposed that we should change our system and move them into the older group at the beginning of Year 6, giving them a year before they leave primary stage education. This would give them the opportunity to form friendships with the older children before the change of school occurred. Those who had already made the move from primary to secondary education could encourage the younger ones and pass on tips and wisdom and give general support.

We listened to Matt and made changes accordingly and he became our transition worker. This also required Matt to be committed to the older Kidz Klub group so that we could mind the gap between churched and unchurched children, extending discipleship opportunities to all.

He developed an existing discipleship course into a programme called Identity which became our main teaching tool for this crossover age group of children in Year 6 through to Year 8. It was aimed at bringing churched and unchurched young people together and being a bridge between Kidz Klub and our youth discipleship groups. Its vision was to give the young people a foundation of faith, looking at topics like, why did Jesus die for them, the Trinity, the gifts and power of the Holy Spirit, worship, witnessing and prayer. A pack was developed to accompany the course, which the diocese has since adopted and published for wider use.

An important role in leadership lies in recognising gaps in our provision. A few years ago, we realised that a separate discipleship group was needed for those aged seventeen plus, and so we formed Script. Pippa and I hosted this in our home on a Sunday evening and it gave us connection with this life-giving and strategic group. When some started to move away to university or college, we tried to keep up the practice of visiting them during their first year. It all contributes to earthing the idea of church as family and the value of discipling through relationship. Later we were able to pass this group on to Rich and Eleanor. During her time as our youth worker, Eleanor had focused particularly on mentoring our older young people and this seemed a natural progression.

An important aspect in discipling young people is releasing them into their call and vision. It's more than simply giving them jobs to do – although that can serve as a helpful start in awakening desire, awareness of gifting and sense of call. In 2010, Juliette and Hannah had come to see me, asking if they could hold a service run by the young people on a Sunday evening. We already had a Sunday evening service in place, so it was a straightforward enough decision to make available one Sunday a term. It was somewhat provocatively called Taking Back Sunday (TBS), and the young people duly did. It was a catalyst for our young people growing into leadership roles. It discipled young people into all aspects of doing 'church': welcome, hospitality, sound, visuals, band, preaching and praying for others. Quite simply, the young people did everything.

Stretching our comfort zone is always good, and enabling young people to take risks, to step out with the safety net of accountability and support has borne much fruit. It proved to be just the sort of challenge the young people needed and it has been extraordinary to see their gifts and ministries grow. I have now lost track of the number of worship leaders who have emerged through the young people over the years. It has also laid the foundation for the way in which we now have a much more integrated worship team of all ages on Sunday mornings, which reflects the demographic of the worshipping community.

Over time, TBS lapsed into a service that was led and organised by the youth workers rather more than the young people. After attending Soul Survivor in 2019, our young people came back energised to take more responsibility for making this their own and it was relaunched as Focus. One of their passions was to make more space for the Holy Spirit to move and for young people to be leading the whole church into encounter with God. One of the aspects that has been so encouraging to see is the way in which the whole church community, young and old, comes to these Sunday evenings. Perhaps initially they came primarily to support the young people. Now they come with a real sense of expectation that they will encounter God for themselves through the worship, teaching and testimony of young people living their lives for Jesus.

We have organised mission weeks to give opportunities for our young people to engage in social action. Typically, we would gather young people in the mornings for teaching, worship and ministry, and then in the afternoons they were sent out as the mission team to some of our local communities. They were involved in practical activities such as litter picking, sharing testimony, praying for people and anything else that came their way. It is the Jesus way of discipleship – throw them in at the deep end and watch them swim!

It is a challenge to keep running all of these activities. There are times when we have had to amalgamate groups when team was depleted. We would have loved to be able to regularly run a supervised crèche on Sunday mornings. In our experience, parents with preschool children are so appreciative of this; knowing their children are being safely looked after enables Mum or Dad to enjoy the teaching and fellowship uninterrupted. However, our ability to do this has been at best intermittent. Everything we do is entirely dependent on having a team and a leader available to organise it. What we can't resource, we can't provide.

We are also committed to supporting others. The Fountain of Life is a member of the New Wine family of churches and, as part of our commitment to New Wine, Maryanne and Matt (Beckett) coordinate the support given to kids' workers across the eastern region. They were invited to lead the Boulder Gang programme at one of the New Wine Summer Gathering weeks. Boulder Gang is for ten- to eleven-year-olds and there are usually around 650 participating children.

Matt and Maryanne were used to leading holiday clubs in excess of 100, and leading school assemblies of much larger groups than this, but it was still a huge step up – it felt like an honour and privilege for them to do this, but daunting nonetheless. For one thing, it would need us to take a huge team from the church. Would we have enough? How many would step up and say, 'Yes, count me in'? In all, we would need a team of around 120 and, amazingly, half of them came from our church. We provided key members of the core group, most of whom had full-time jobs and took annual leave in order to be at the event. As our commitment to run this programme was for at least three years, we needed this core group to commit to that time period.

It has been thrilling to see the way in which the team rose to the challenge and excelled, and how year on year the delivery became more and more amazing. The organisation was greatly helped by Becky, a natural administrator, stepping in to support Maryanne and Matt by doing what she does best. But so many others stepped in to critical roles. We find so often that when people step up to 'more' there is an increase to their level of faith, giftedness, confidence and anointing. This comes back home with them and helps continue to strengthen and build up the local church.

I would strongly encourage those of you who lead churches to encourage members of your church to serve at events like New Wine. The exposure to something larger reaps so many benefits back home in the encouragement, confidence and gifting of the team through the rest of the year.

There was a cost. The Fountain of Life effectively became the lead church for delivering Boulder Gang. It did cost us financially, it required staff time, it stretched our teams – particularly because we were still committed to running two holiday clubs in the summer – and we had to build in time to focus on preparation and training during the year. Running a whole programme like this probably has a season of life attached to it, but its knock-on effect in building team and growth in gifting and confidence is off the scale.

As part of fulfilling our responsibility to the diocese as a resource church, Maryanne and Matt organise an annual children's workers training day on behalf of the diocese, which is delivered in partnership with New Wine. Maryanne also trains volunteers in other churches to deliver CAP Money, envisions schools and churches about the value of TLG and raises up others to deliver Christmas and Easter Experiences in schools. All of this helps us fulfil our call to encourage, empower and equip the wider Church, putting tools in their hands that enable us all to see the kingdom come.

Let me conclude this chapter in perhaps an unexpected way, by talking about the older people in our church. It sometimes surprises people when they visit us to see the breadth of age range represented in the average gathered congregation, and in particular, the significant proportion of those over the age of sixty. The preconception that can be cast over a church with a modern, contemporary style is that lots of young people and children, loud music, drums and guitars do not mix with older people – and vice versa. In our experience, this is simply not true. Young people value the prayers, wisdom, love and support of older people, who often take on the role of spiritual mothers and fathers in the church as well as being the backbone of many of our teams. It is, of course, a reciprocal relationship. The older generation love to see the vivacity that young people and children provide simply by their presence(!) and to see the baton of faith being passed on.

Family means building a church for all ages. Ensuring that we are meeting the needs of children and young people does not need to be done at the expense of engaging with the older generation. The 'golden thread' principle applies to them too.

6
Releasing the Gold

From him the whole body, joined and held together by
every supporting ligament, grows and builds itself up in
love, as each part does its work.
(Ephesians 4:16)

We know that the body of Christ is one of the metaphors or pictures used particularly by Paul (1 Corinthians 12:12-27; Ephesians 1:22-23; 4:15-16) to describe the extraordinary potential of the Church. But experiencing this in an empowered and supported way is not always our personal experience. In 1 Corinthians 12, the way this is intended to work in practice is likened to the human body. There is interdependence between the members. Just as in natural life, if a particular part of the human body is absent or not able to function fully, then the life of the whole body suffers and is somehow incomplete. No part is superior or inferior to the other. As Paul says, 'if the ear should say, "Because I am not an eye, I do not belong to the body," it would not for that reason stop being part of the body' (1 Corinthians 12:16). Equally, 'The eye cannot say to the hand, "I don't need you!"' (1 Corinthians 12:21). Similarly, within the body of Christ each of us has a vital role to play: some are more visible than others, some are seen more often than others, some hold more prominent positions than others, but none is to be seen as more important or significant than the others. Each individual has unique purpose, worth, identity and value.

In his letter to the Ephesian church, Paul adjusts the focus of the same metaphor to emphasise that Christ is the head of the body – the Church belongs to Him. The Church is held together by its relationship to the person of Jesus Christ, empowered by His Spirit, embraced in the love of the Father and designed to reflect the glory of God to the society and world around us. Our purpose is to be obedient to Him and represent Him in the world.

Sometimes, church can look as if its primary focus is to gather people around the vision of the leader. Leaders need to define vision, but our vision as leaders at the Fountain of Life has been to see the people we lead released into their gifts, ministries, vision and call. Often this has in turn shaped 'our' vision and multiplied the direction in which the church has travelled. It has produced a dynamic in the church that is empowering and produces life.

We are all called to 'encourage one another' (1 Thessalonians 5:11), but leaders have a particular role in releasing and equipping each person to play their part according to their specific gifts, ministries and callings. Paul specifically defines the purpose of those who are called apostles, prophets, evangelists, pastors and teachers as being to prepare God's people for 'works of service, so that the body of Christ may be built up until we all reach unity in the faith and in the knowledge of the Son of God and become mature, attaining to the whole measure of the fullness of Christ' (Ephesians 4:11-13). I have come to see this as suggesting that my fruitfulness is measured not by how apostolic I have been as a leader, or how prophetically I have led, but how intentional I have been in raising up others by envisioning, teaching and training and then releasing them into their 'works of service'. The goal of a good teacher is to raise up others who will go further. This applies to us all. It's not about 'my' ministry as a prophet or as a pastor. It's about how many others are following in my footsteps. Who do I encourage to go further than I have? Do I give them opportunities to grow? Am I prepared to take risks that might lead to apparent failure? Being a church leader was never intended to be about me – some kind of one-man show to entertain others. We have the opportunity to build a platform upon which others can stand. The gifts and ministries are given in abundance so that all get to play.

As Francis Chan put it:

> Long gone are the days when I am content with a bunch of people who sing loud, don't divorce, and give to missions. I now want to know I can drop off any member of my church in a city and that person could grow in Jesus, make disciples, and start a church. My faith in the Holy Spirit's power convinces me this is possible. It is in our very DNA. We all have been given a spirit of courage and the power to do beyond what we can imagine. We must train our people to be independently dependent on the Holy Spirit.[95]

We have intentionally sought to develop a culture in which people can flourish, and there are some things we have done to help to bring this about.

We have encouraged people to serve out of vision and call rather than simply volunteer to meet a need. Of course, response to need can be part of the discernment process, but the more a person is serving out of a sense of 'this is what I am made for' and a response to the Spirit's enabling and empowering, the more fruitful and fulfilling will be the outcome in terms of discipleship and growth – both for the person and for the community.

We have to be prepared to take risks with people, and that includes giving them the freedom to fail. I remember a young woman who sang in our worship team on a Sunday morning for

---

[95] Francis Chan, *Letters to the Church* (Colorado Springs, CA: David C Cook, 2018), p120.

the first time. She had a beautiful voice and was clearly at home and comfortable in the team and on the platform. When asked whether she had ever done anything like this before, her response was, 'No, this is the first time I felt as if I had the freedom to fail.'

Creating a safe place for the exercise of gifts and ministries helps people to realise their full potential as members of the body of Christ. Developing and pastoring a church in which everyone is encouraged to discover and exercise their own ministry is a balance between giving people enough encouragement and space to grow while also providing appropriate accountability.

Releasing people requires us to be intentional about training people. It's vital that we teach well so that people are not 'uninformed' (1 Corinthians 12:1) about spiritual gifts and ministries, but instead understand what they are and how they work and have opportunities to put them into practice. Alongside this, we need to help people discover their vocation and calling.

In any healthy church there are new people joining. We are mindful of the need to mind the gap between their experience and the vision and values of the church, and especially to teach about life in the Spirit and living out a kingdom lifestyle. There are various courses and training days that we have regularly run in exploring these issues. Our Kingdom Life course seeks to establish a secure biblical foundation for how to live in the reality of the kingdom and gives plenty of opportunity to learn how to practise a supernatural lifestyle. It seeks to increase people's confidence in hearing God's voice for themselves and to engage in the supernatural ministry of the kingdom. We cover such topics as being filled with the Spirit, developing the fruit of the Spirit (character) and gifts of the Spirit (competency), including prophecy and healing, as well as looking at practical ways in which we share our faith with others.

Another area of teaching we have found to be helpful is based around the acronym SHAPE, which has been helpful to us in the process of discerning call and vision. This was originally taught by Rick Warren, senior pastor of Saddleback Church in Southern California.[96] It explores five key elements that shape a person. These are: the person's *spiritual gifts,* the things God has specifically given to them; looking at what their *heart* is stirred by, their passions, desires, the things they love to do; paying attention to their natural *abilities,* the things they cannot help but be good at; taking note of how their *personality* is wired; and the *experiences* – both good and bad – they have through their education, employment and other events of life. Recently, a young man emailed me to say how much this had helped him at a point when he was taking some decisions on his future career. He had kept his notes for several years before applying them at that particular time.

Before we move on, here are a couple of significant examples of people being released into serving and the blessing this has had upon the life of the church and our ability to be missionary.

A few years ago I was concerned that our carol service was very predictable and lacked creativity. I was feeling that we were missing an opportunity to engage with those who came, and were not attracting enough people outside the church to come in the first place. Christmas is a major opportunity for the church to engage with community and, perhaps feeling that the depiction of the Fountain of Life as 'a missionary congregation of the Church of England' gave us added responsibility to be more cutting edge in our approach, I decided that we needed to do more.

I knew that Rachel, a member of our congregation, had trained as an actress and had served with the Christian theatre company Riding Lights for a year. So, I decided to have a conversation with her. People were used to my approaching them with an idea, so she received me with a certain degree of

---

[96] Outlined, for example, in *The Purpose Driven Church* by Rick Warren. Copyright © 1995 by Rick Warren. Used by permission of Zondervan. www.zondervan.com (accessed 20th January 2021).

caution. However, she very graciously agreed to help, and our carol service that year featured a puppet sketch and was supported by some video clips punctuated by readings, carols and a short talk. It was very well received and seemed to be a step in the right direction. Over the next couple of years we built on this as the pattern.

Then one day it was Rachel's turn to take me aside and start outlining her thoughts about what we could do for the following Christmas. Effectively this required me to delegate authority and therefore control to Rachel for the carol service. Rachel did not disappoint. What she came up with included a dramatised working of the nativity. It featured puppets, songs and drama, as well as traditional carols. We let all of this presentation speak for itself and simply closed our time together with an invitation for people to invite Jesus into their lives and consider attending Alpha. Afterwards, there was plenty of conversation over seasonal refreshments.

I also asked Rachel to perform various sketches and dramas during services and to lead one or two all-age events on other occasions through the year. Through this she built up a team of budding actors whom she took under her wing. She invested time in them and provided training in the foundational principles of performing, wrote amazing scripts and inspired everyone's confidence.

As often happens in the kingdom, a seed grows into something amazing and beyond our expectations. Rachel came to see me again. By this time it was me who was cautious. She proposed a Christmas event which came to be called Christmas Alive. This would be an enhanced dramatic presentation of the nativity, with some twists. It would require a live donkey and special effects, and alongside the production was a Bethlehem village recreated as close to first-century authenticity as our car park would allow. We said 'yes', and Christmas Alive was born. Our first Christmas Alive was held in 2015 and was so well received that we repeated it, with an expanded village which now included pottery, carpentry, a census-taker, spices and traditional foods, dance, and Hebrew songs, all of which created an authentic Middle Eastern atmosphere.

However, after a couple of years at least two problems arose. The first was that we simply could not accommodate everyone. It was clear that Christmas Alive needed space in which to expand and grow. The second issue was that, somewhat ironically, given the original intent, we had lost our carol service and replaced it with something else which, while rooted in Scripture, increasingly had become more of a production and performance. Great as this 'something else' was, we needed our carol service back but without losing Christmas Alive.

There was a simple solution to this second issue. We resolved it by deciding to hold a rather more traditional carol service of lessons and carols on the following Sunday. This was an altogether more peaceful affair and is much loved. We would be the poorer without it as it affords more time to hear the timeless truth of the Christmas story simply told through reading the Scriptures and singing more of those much-loved carols which often contain such very good theology.

It was Rachel and her Christmas Alive team who came up with the solution to the first issue, which on the surface was simply to run multiple presentations of the same event. At the same time, though, her vision for the scale of the event was enlarging. She had the idea for telling the story of the birth of Jesus through the lens of another popular Christmas tale: *A Christmas Carol*.[97] So the Christmas Alive production was subtitled: *Scrooge Reworked.* Instead of Scrooge being visited by three spirits, he would be visited by the Holy Spirit, who would accompany him on visits to the past, present and future. The performance concluded with Scrooge's heart being transformed through his encounters with the Spirit. It was a genius concept, with an amazing script and fantastic musical accompaniment. Our son, Simon, worked with Rachel on the musical side,

---

[97] *A Christmas Carol* is a novella by Charles Dickens, first published in London by Chapman & Hall in 1843.

writing music to accompany Rachel's lyrics, and the production was born. Scrooge was played by Steve, his younger self by Isaac and Sam, Bob Cratchit by Caleb, and the Holy Spirit by Karen. So many others stepped up in character to play their part. No one had done anything quite like this before, but they all excelled in their respective roles.

In the first year of this production, in 2018, we held two performances, and the following year we were compelled to hold four. Many commented on its professionalism and high standards. Someone put into words what most felt: 'Christmas just isn't Christmas without Christmas Alive.' People were going up to Rachel at the end and sayings things like, 'Every word was directed to me. Scrooge is me,' and Rachel was able to lead them in prayer. In the course of time some became Christians and joined our church. Christmas Alive is now promoted across the region as a 'must-see' Christmas event. In its last year before Covid, our regional newspaper, the *Eastern Daily Press*, rated it second only to seeing the Queen at Sandringham in the top ten Christmas attractions! The story continues to develop, as a person who came along to see one of the performances is now seeking to make a way for us to take the production into prisons.

A huge team of 100 made Christmas Alive happen. It required muscles to erect the village, electricians, caterers, welcomers, musicians, actors, ushers, stewards, coffee and tea-makers, administrators, painters, scenery-makers, designers and those willing to serve in whatever way was needed. In order to release gifts and ministries, you do need opportunities to serve. Events like Christmas Alive are worth their weight in gold alone for the value that they are in releasing so much treasure in those who make it happen, building team and creating family.

The second illustrative story of people being released into their SHAPE is one that has enabled us as a church to make an effective response in the arena of mental health. This was a topic of interest to me; I had personal experience as a teenager, as my mother suffered from depression at times. Looking back, there were certainly moments when it felt as if I was her primary source of emotional support. As a leader I was also aware of how important it is for each of us to be attentive to managing well our own mental and emotional health.

Pete Scazzero's book *The Emotionally Healthy Church*[98] is a really helpful read on this subject. He explores a biblical perspective, rooted in an understanding of the first couple of chapters of Genesis. This establishes that we are created in the image of God as integrated mind, body, soul and spirit people with the capacity to think, feel and act. He then explores six principles of growing an emotionally healthy church. We are often more aware, skilled and able to manage our physical health than our emotional or mental well-being. In the film *First Man*,[99] which is based on the Apollo 11 space mission and subsequent moon landings, Neil Armstrong is portrayed as finding it easier to navigate the journey from planet Earth to the moon and back than to face the emotional journey of pain and grief following the loss of his daughter.

At one of our staff meetings in 2016, we had initiated a conversation about our response as a church to issues of mental health. At this meeting we all agreed that we desired the Fountain of Life to be a safe place for those who wrestle with mental health issues in any form, and for that to happen we needed a culture of openness and vulnerability and to release the stigma that is often attached to Christians who struggle in this area of health and well-being. We were also very aware that as a staff team we lacked the expertise to provide the 'safe place' in which this could be explored, and in particular needed to have the right support in place for those who would need further help and support.

It so happened that Elaine had recently moved to the area and joined the Fountain of Life. She was a professional adult, child and adolescent psychotherapeutic counsellor. She was

[98] Peter Scazzero, *The Emotionally Healthy Church* (Grand Rapids, MI: Zondervan, 2015) and also *The Emotionally Healthy Leader* (Grand Rapids, MI: Zondervan, 2015).

[99] *First Man*, Universal Pictures, 2018.

already engaged in much wider conversations geared to forming a Norfolk-wide strategic response to issues of mental health, and was excited about the potential for integrating her faith and a Christian perspective into those conversations. Elaine was willing to coordinate our response. As a first step she organised a Doors of Hope conference about mental health and well-being aimed not just at the Fountain of Life, but also at equipping other churches in the region to be in active partnership alongside statutory and medical agencies. At this conference, Elaine spoke about her vision for the church: 'We believe that Church is well placed to support people with mental ill-health, to challenge stigma and shame, and to offer hope and resilience skills.'

Through Elaine we actively supported the Norfolk Children and Young People Mental Health Summit, Looking Forward, in September 2017, bringing together a range of professional organisations and the local churches. The first Doors of Hope conference was held on 17th November 2018 and 170 people attended. This became an annual event. Maureen stepped in to help Elaine with the administration of the event. Like all of the other activities of the church, we depend upon lots of others who work behind the scenes in sacrificial and supportive ways.

We have often been blessed by wonderfully gifted church administrators – Becky, Dave and now Karen. The gift of administration is so significant in turning vision into action. The Greek word used (*kubermesis*) (1 Corinthians 12:28) literally means to steer, a word that in New Testament times was used in the context of a captain at the helm of the ship. A helpful image. Just as the ship needs to be steered into position to catch the wind in its sails, so the gift of administration helps the church harness and lean into the power of the wind of the Spirit. Administration is a leadership gift and when it serves alongside the apostolic and prophetic, it releases the potential of the vision in a way that would not otherwise be fulfilled. It releases others into their gifts and ministries. It's a wonderful gift that equips and empowers the body of Christ to achieve more than it otherwise would.

We have found running the Alpha course to be a great way of involving people. It requires gifts of hosting, hospitality, welcome, catering, leading small groups and delivering the talks. It is also such an encouraging place, where people are coming to faith and growing in their discipleship.

Reg and Christine moved into the area and Christine started coming to church as she was looking for something similar to her previous one. When I introduced myself to Reg, his hasty response was, 'I am only here for my wife.' Reg was not an atheist, but he was very sceptical about the Christian faith. He did, however, have a wife and son who had been praying for him over many years. Reg was struck by the warmth of our welcome, made new friends and was impressed by the extent of the youth work within the church. He found himself coming along regularly. Then he decided to do Alpha, and during the course he began to come to terms with all his past misgivings and, for the first time, invited Jesus into his life. He went on to do the Kingdom Life course to be equipped in praying for people and exercising the gifts of the Spirit.

Sometime later his son, Jack, emailed me to say:

> It has been such a joy to see my dad growing in his faith and discovery of Jesus' love for him. After so many years of prayer it moves me to tears of happiness. My lead elder at church once preached a sermon entitled 'The Church isn't like a family; it is a family'. This just seems so evident in the Fountain of Life family which has welcomed my parents so well.

Roy came on the Alpha course. He had experienced pain and damage as a result of broken family relationships which had left him feeling hurt and betrayed. He was filled with the Holy Spirit, received healing and restoration of his faith and 'experienced the love and friendship of God and my brothers and sisters within the family of God'. Empowered by this love, he and his wife, Vee, support a nearby night shelter for the homeless.

Nicole had been dating Luke since they met at high school aged fourteen. Nicole was a Christian but, up until this point, God had not featured in Luke's life. Luke spent most weekends at Nicole's house where the conversation would often flow about faith and God, especially over Sunday lunch, and Luke occasionally went to church with Nicole's family.

Then Nicole and her family joined the Fountain and Luke came along more often. He and Nicole became engaged and did a marriage preparation course with us. I agreed to preside over their wedding on condition that Luke would then do the Alpha course. Following their wedding in 2016 they attended church regularly and, about a year later, Luke and Nicole came on Alpha. From the very first session, Luke began to have his questions and doubts about faith, evil in the world and free will addressed.

Early on in the course, his nan passed away. This was hard for Luke, as they had been particularly close since childhood. One evening, as he was walking back from work, Luke felt a hand rest on his shoulder and he sensed God say, 'Your nan is with me. It's your journey now, Luke. Off you go.' This both comforted and reassured him. He had often heard stories of others who had experienced similar life-changing moments. He had always thought to himself, 'Is it really that simple?' Now Luke had his own story to tell and his faith soared.

Luke was baptised in September 2018. Jo, Nicole's mum, had prayed that her daughter would marry a Christian and her prayers were now answered.

On the day of his baptism, a member of the church, Connie, came to welcome him into the family of the church. She told him that she saw him 'standing on a hill and there's a sunrise behind you. You have wings.' Luke reminded her that two years earlier, on the very first day that Luke had walked into the church, Connie had told him, 'I see you standing on a hill and there's a sunrise behind you.' Spot the difference! Since the first picture, Luke had formed wings. He was ready to fly.

Size and model of group plays an essential part in creating space for people to 'fly' within the body of Christ in exercising their gifts and ministries. It is undoubtedly true that the way we tend to do church on a Sunday restricts the number of players. This has certainly been true in our Fountain context, with the average Sunday congregation being 200. At this kind of size, there is a limited number who will feel competent and confident about participating from the front. We have still seen a significant number of people raised up and released into position. We have several worship leaders, a team of seven who regularly preach and those who serve in less visible ways when we meet together – sound desk, visuals, refreshments, welcomers, prayer ministry team. It's fantastic and we have very solidly moved away from a 'one leader' focus.[100] However, we do need alternative-size groupings in which to meet if we are to unlock the full potential of the body of Christ. These give us the building blocks to work with in releasing and growing people into the things God has for them, and it moves more people from being spectators to active participants.

Home groups are great places for gifts to be explored. I have seen several worship leaders emerge who have begun somewhat gingerly by picking up their guitar and leading a small group of people in singing a worship song or hymn. I remember being in one such group where we sang the same song several times for several weeks before the repertoire expanded. It's what you do in a family. Our grandchildren went with their parents to lunch recently with some friends who are professional musicians. They allowed the children, at the time aged six and four, to play a small violin and trumpet. The outcome, though apparently not entirely unpleasing to the ear, was probably not at a concert

---

[100] Since the restrictions imposed by Covid, the strength of the preaching, worship leading and technical team has enriched our capacity to respond well online.

performance level. But I'm sure that the result was greeted with rapturous delight. It's a bit like that in a small group when someone steps out to do something they haven't done before. It's family and a safe place to explore.

Whether it's leading a Bible study, picking up a guitar, reading a passage of Scripture or praying out loud for the first time, it's a place where we can discern gifting and grow in competency and confidence. I can well remember praying my very first prayer out loud in a small group. I had it all worked out, but it took me a very long time to have the courage to verbalise it. So long that others would fill the silence before I mustered the courage to speak, often praying the very words I would have prayed! But eventually one week the silence continued for long enough to enable me to finally pluck up the necessary 'courage' to deliver my prayer. I really can't remember it very much, but I do remember my nervousness and cold sweat, which was entirely disproportionate to its significance.

However, even when we have grown confident in a group of around ten, which is the typical size of a home group, it is then still a huge step up to offer our gifting in the 200-plus setting. Gathering in a crowd on a Sunday certainly gave us the value of celebration and the dynamic of numbers, but it was much easier for people to remain anonymous and harder to release them into their full discipleship potential. At the same time, our smaller home groups, so vital with all their benefits of intimacy and accountability, did not appeal to everyone and could become closed to others joining. There was a value in having something in-between.[101]

---

[101] I have been writing this book during the Covid-19 pandemic, which has enforced a shift away from gathered church to our homes, and meeting in smaller groups via our screens. Pippa and I have been leading a small group online, which numbers twenty-five. We may not be able to physically meet together, but we can still worship, study the Bible and pray for one another. We can still be open to the Holy Spirit to move and speak. And we can still have fun with online quizzes and games.

This fits with insights gleaned from the world of sociology that identifies four sociological spaces or sizes of meeting together: intimate space, personal space, social space and public space.[102] Against this understanding, our Life groups with two or three people meeting together provided intimate space, home groups represented personal space and our Sunday celebrations the public space. This left 'social space', which requires a group size in the order of twenty-five to fifty. As observed by Mike Breen and Bob and Mary Hopkins, this 'provides a social context with good access to leaders for everyone; the potential for all to contribute in interactive gatherings; the facility for knowing everyone and missing them when absent; and the ability for all to own the vision and have a strong sense of belonging to the group'.[103]

As a new Christian I had experienced something of this in the model of home groups and pastorates at HTB. We would meet in home groups fortnightly, and on the alternate weeks home groups would come together to form pastorates. Each pastorate was typically made up of five or six home groups and, in practice, each time they met, around thirty people would come together. Their purpose was largely pastoral but it gave an opportunity for gifts to be exercised in a larger setting. I remember giving my very first talk to a pastorate, and it felt very different from leading a Bible study in the smaller setting. At the time, my employment was within the sphere of redundancy counselling, outplacement services and headhunting and I had also done some work in pursuing a biblical perspective on issues of work and employment. My lay pastor had wanted to give me the opportunity to speak. So it was a wise move for him to ask me to speak on a biblical view of work. He gave me a subject about which he knew I would have something to say – at least, he hoped I would!

[102] Bob Hopkins and Mike Breen, *Clusters: Creative Mid-Sized Missional Communities* (Greenville, SC: 3DM Publications, 2007), p23; see www.3dmovements.com (accessed 13th May 2021).
[103] Ibid, p18.

We explored this pastorate model earlier in our journey at the Fountain. For a season, we combined our existing home groups to form two pastorates, allocating five or six home groups to each. Paul and Julia were appointed as leaders of the two pastorates. They did a great job of supporting the home group leaders and releasing gifts and ministries. Each pastorate met monthly and home groups met as normal on the other weeks. This pattern continued for a couple of years but, in the end, attendance at the pastorates dwindled. I think a combination of factors contributed, but perhaps the main one was that they did not have a purposefulness about them that sufficiently gripped the imagination of the people. I suspect it was the outward focus that was lacking. At the time, we were still small enough on a Sunday for people to know one another, and with the small groups functioning well, the value of yet another pastoral grouping was diminished.

Nonetheless, our growing understanding of the value of this kind of 'mid-sized community', and the experience of our pastorates, played a key part in laying the foundation for what was to come. They have been part of our journey which has led to the development of missional communities, and it is this area of our life together to which we turn next.

7
Missional Communities

The LORD had said to Abram, 'Go from your country,
your people and your father's household to the land I will
show you.'
(Genesis 12:1)

At the beginning of 2012, Alan came to see me, as he felt the
Lord was speaking to us through Deuteronomy 1:6-8:

> You have stayed long enough at this mountain. Break
> camp and advance into the hill country of the Amorites;
> go to all the neighbouring peoples in the Arabah, in the
> mountains, in the western foothills, in the Negev and
> along the coast, to the land of the Canaanites and to
> Lebanon, as far as the great river, the Euphrates. See, I
> have given you this land. Go in and take possession of
> the land that the LORD swore he would give to your
> fathers – to Abraham, Isaac and Jacob – and to their
> descendants after them.

There are not many hills in Norfolk but it seemed an apposite
'now' word for us. By this time our membership was hovering
around the 250 mark, which exactly matched our seating
capacity. In practice we were usually about 200 strong on a
Sunday morning but even so we were looking full, and it was

very clear that we needed a different model of gathered church if we were to continue to see significant growth. We were aware of the insights gained in church growth research, which informed us that once a building is 80 per cent full, further growth is unlikely. I was not enamoured with the idea of embarking on creating another church building – you can never build a church big enough to contain Him. So, something needed to change.

To draw on an analogy from the retail industry, and supermarkets in particular, we could either multiply our checkouts – our services – or our locations. It was hard to see how we could repeat our morning service. We did not have the resources to run multiple programmes for children and young people and, given our deeply rural location and the gathered nature of our congregation, having enough time for more than one morning service was problematic. Multiplying locations seemed to be a more realistic option and fitted with the nature of kingdom growth (Matthew 13) – after all, God is a God of multiplication.[104] However, we felt called to do more than simply replicate the way we did church on a Sunday in other places – becoming some sort of multi-site church.

Alan's insight from the book of Deuteronomy confirmed the direction that we were already exploring. We had become aware of the value of 'social space' referred to in the previous chapter and recognised that our pastorates had needed the zest of mission in order to flourish. We needed to be led by mission.

We were also aware of the limitations of the 'attractional' ('come to us') model of church for engaging in mission. The mission imperative required us to adopt a 'go to them' attitude. We lived in an increasingly diverse culture with lots of different people groups and networks. We needed to be building bridges to reach these diverse networks and neighbourhoods, and that required a multiplicity of approaches. After all, we had been established as a network church in recognition that people's

---

[104] See for example Genesis 9:7; Mark 4:8.

relationships are formed around work, leisure, lifestyle, interests, communities. We needed to become more imaginative and creative in reaching out to these groups. We were looking for ways of multiplying mission and becoming more fruitful.

There were a number of factors at play in our search for the way forward. We wanted to send people out creatively, but how? As we explored the answer to this question, we discovered various models and forms of language in churches that were further ahead than us in investigating how to engage in this way.

St Andrew's Chorleywood described its mid-sized groups as Lifeboats.[105] It is helpful language in generating a sense of urgency: people are in danger of being swept away and need rescuing. Out of this some people have developed a helpful acronym which added value to our thinking. These groups are *lightweight* – not encumbered by staffing costs, buildings or programmes; manned by an *inspired* crew who share a common vision and call; are *fit* for purpose and *easy* to join, ideally gaining leaders from the community they are seeking to serve; are *buoyant* and *on* the move; *attached* to a lifeboat station and they *take* risks – they are manoeuvrable and can be where they are needed quickly.

Much of this language resonated with our vision. We were up for taking risks and releasing people to lead mission initiatives that would reach people with the gospel and grow, but we also recognised the importance of keeping them connected – or attached – to the hub of the Fountain of Life for resources and support. Many fledgling church plants die through lack of back-up. We were looking for 'church' to emerge out of the mission engagement, being open to how the Holy Spirit was at work in the community to which we were sent rather than parachuting in with our pre-formed ideas.

---

[105] You can read more of its story in Mark Stibbe and Andrew Williams, *Breakout: One Church's Amazing Story of Growth Through Mission-Shaped Communities* (Milton Keynes: Authentic, 2008).

St Thomas Crookes[106] referred to its mid-sized communities as 'Clusters', using language coined by Bob and Mary Hopkins, who lead a church-planting organisation, Anglican Church Planting Initiatives (ACPI).[107] Other churches, such as Holy Trinity Leicester under John McGinley's leadership, tapped into the language of missional communities.[108] The words may vary but they all had something in common: organised with a missional purpose in mind and typically thirty to fifty-ish in size (although it's purpose rather than size that is the more important characteristic). Usually they met in 'third places': places that were neither the church nor the home, but places that the communities would recognise as their own – a pub, village hall, community centre or school hall, for example.

We had already begun to use the language of missional community, and in the end it was this language that stuck. It resonated well with the language of our original call to be a missionary congregation. It also gave us a helpful framework and vocabulary that created a unity in the church between the old and the new. This language enabled us to create a culture that would release vision for new initiatives to begin, as well as to embrace our existing mission-focused activities.

Andrea readily caught the idea of her First Steps preschool and associated Noah's Ark, the parent and toddlers group, as being a missional community. Andrea's vision and practice was already missional in reaching out to whole families.

Good Companions, which reached out to older people, was effectively functioning as a missional community too, and its leaders, Susan and Jean, identified with the language. Its roots lay with Grace, a lady recently widowed, who had reached out

---

[106] stthomascrookes.org/about/how-we-do-church/ (accessed 27th January 2021).

[107] acpi.org.uk (accessed 2nd February 2021).

[108] John McGinley, *Mission-Shaped Grace Missional Practices for Missional Disciples* (East Malling: River Publishing & Media Ltd, 2017); John McGinley, *Mission-Shaped Living* (Colorado Springs, CO: David C Cook, 2020).

to those in a similar position with God's love and compassion. This had grown into a monthly Sunday afternoon tea for those aged sixty-plus – a significant age group in our surrounding area, often isolated and lonely, experiencing relational poverty. Even though Good Companions met in our church building, it was missional in nature and purpose. Once a month two minibuses set out to pick them all up (including Zimmer frames et al), with many others chauffeured in, and regularly between fifty and seventy people would gather for afternoon tea; entertainment would be provided in the form of quizzes, life stories, music and choirs. A familiar hymn would be sung, prayers would be said and there would be informal conversations about faith. It has been a lifeline for many, providing much-needed comfort, companionship, conversation and fun.

It is 'church' in all but name. On one occasion, as part of a mission week, I went door-knocking in one of our local market towns and I asked one resident the usual questions, one of which was connected to church.

'Oh,' came the reply, 'I come to your church.'

'Really?' I said. 'I'm so sorry, but I didn't recognise you.'

'I come to your monthly Sunday afternoon tea,' she said. It was then that I realised she considered Good Companions to be her 'church'. In due time she died and left a legacy to the Fountain of Life – she considered herself to be one of the family.

One of the longer-term tests of viability we apply for any ministry or activity within the church is continuity of leadership. We encourage all the teams to be looking out for the next person to follow in their footsteps. In due course, Maureen took on the leadership of this team as they continued to reach this older generation with the gospel through kindness and companionship supported by hymns and testimony.

Bezalel is a group focused around the skills of sewing, embroidery and banner-making. It was started by Enid and, after her death, was taken on by Susan and Sandra. This group has provided the creative ideas and banners for a sermon series on the Beatitudes and the 'I Am' descriptions of Jesus, as well as much seasonal material. Alongside this, they have a lot of fun working on their own sewing and knitting projects and organising day trips and the occasional coach holiday.

Our Kidz Klubs readily bought into the language of missional community, as did our youth group. So it did indeed prove to be an inclusive language to use in bringing our existing missional activities together around a common vision with a shared vocabulary. At the same time it released new initiatives, which I shall come to later. Just to be clear, though, let's first explore what we mean by missional community.

As the name suggests, a missional community is a community that defines itself by mission. It is led by those with a vision and intent to connect with those who do not necessarily have a relationship with God. This connection may be through a shared interest, a local neighbourhood, a desire to reach a specific age group, a particular social need or a work-related group, or may be built around any other connection that brings people together.

What is needed to make a missional community effective? It is a community that is first and foremost defined by a missional purpose. It requires a leader, ideally more than one (Luke 10:1), with vision and the ability to communicate that vision and build a team around them. The heart of the vision must be to reach those who are outside the church and, in recruiting a team, it is good to look for those who are able to relate well to not-yet Christians. Team is essential in providing the support and encouragement necessary to persevere and to release the diversity of gifting and abilities necessary if the work is to flourish.

When the group is meeting in a place outside the church, there needs to be favour from those in authority which gives the team the right to be there. The 'person of peace' principle drawn from the sending of the seventy-two in Luke's Gospel is a very helpful one to hold on to as a key to unlocking a mission context

(Luke 10:6[109]). This encourages us to focus on praying and looking for those who are open and receptive to the team; those who welcome us, listen to our voice and open their doors – and hearts – to us. This also serves to emphasise how our missionary journey needs to be birthed and rooted in prayer, listening to the chosen context as well as to the Father.

Here at the Fountain, we have applied great flexibility in the way a missional community is formed. It needs to be missional in purpose, but there is no fixed template: numbers vary; the place in which they meet is negotiable – some even meet in the worship centre if that is the best location; some meet weekly, others monthly and one or two even less regularly; some meet on Sundays and others during the week. However, we do need consistency in our vision, core values and vocabulary, and use the acronym FIRE to help provide some cohesion and clarity in forming and communicating this.

Family: God is community – Father, Son and Holy Spirit[110] – and the Church is intended to reflect this image and, as the family of God, to be an extension of this community. We applied this value to the whole of the Fountain of Life Church but it should be even more strongly recognisable in the smaller context of our missional communities. The weakness of just having an attractional ('come to us') church model is that it can produce consumer Christians who never mature beyond milk to solid food (Hebrews 5:11-14) and become dependent on the next church programme. A core value of missional communities is releasing more people into exercising their gifts and ministries, giving them the opportunity to grow more quickly than they otherwise might.

Incarnational: We are following in the footsteps of our pioneer, Jesus. He became like us and lived among us.[111] He

---

[109] When the disciples are sent out by Jesus, they are instructed by Jesus to linger in the places where they are welcomed by people of peace. This would be a sign to them of an openness to receiving the gospel.

[110] For example: Genesis 1:26; 1 Corinthians 8:6; 2 Corinthians 3:17.

[111] John 1:14; Philippians 2:7.

143

called people to follow Him and church was formed as they did. The presence and activity of God creates church, not vice versa. We seek to see what God is doing, and join in. Sometimes it feels to me as if church planting can quench what the Spirit is doing if we are not careful to first tune in to how He is already at work. It is all too easy to transport our preconceived ideas of 'church' and expect that model to work in the new context. The emphasis in developing a missional community is to engage with the culture of the place or people group and allow 'church' to emerge out of that process of listening and engagement. It's moving from the 'come to us' focus of attractional church to a 'go and stay' model, allowing church as the Spirit is growing it to emerge. However, the one does not need to be at the expense of the other. The value of each is significantly enhanced when both the 'come' and the 'go' model can be accommodated in the one vision. We need the resource of the gathered so that we may be sent.

Raising leaders: Our job is to 'make disciples'[112] who make disciples who in turn make disciples. Disciples are followers of Jesus and therefore leaders who influence others with the values of the kingdom. A missional community provides a place in which leaders can be multiplied. It provides a safe place in which disciples can be raised up and grow in their character, gifts and abilities, in particular allowing space for the five-fold ministry of apostles, prophets, evangelists, pastors and teachers to grow and flourish (Ephesians 4:11).

Encountering God: This changes everything. The testimony of our lives is the most effective witness to the power of the gospel to bring transformation and release hope. This is not about perfection. Often the gospel is made more clearly known through our weakness, our vulnerability, the issues of life with which we wrestle, the way in which we respond to suffering and disappointment. As we share our lives together in as authentic, open and transparent a way as possible so we build

---

112 Matthew 28:19.

144

bridges of trust with people around us who may then become more open to listening to what we have to say.

So, let's now take a look at some examples of the new initiatives that emerged, particularly looking at those with a geographical focus.

One of our first missional communities of this kind to emerge was Refresh. This was started by Neil and Maryanne with the help at the time of their two teenage daughters, Juliette and Grace. It built on the work of Kidz Klub, which was based at their local primary school. Its principal aim was to reach the families of the children who attended regularly. The monthly visiting gave opportunities for Maryanne and her team to establish good connections with some of these families. The persistence and longevity of their work over the past fifteen years has borne much fruit. They have engaged in different ways over the years. They prayer walked their neighbourhood; engaged in outreaches connected to Hope[113] initiatives; hosted Alpha courses and, for a season, a discipleship group in their home. They are not afraid to stop, regroup and plan again.

Before Covid-19, the main gathering was bi-monthly at lunchtime after the Kidz Klub morning meeting. This meeting was for all the family and they played games, ate together and enjoyed creative activities, an interactive talk, worship and opportunity for conversation and prayer. The aim was to build authentic church there. Some have come to faith and joined our central gathering on a Sunday morning, or a discipleship group. Others are more on the fringe. All are on a journey. A gathering was organised just before Christmas 2019 and eighty-five people came along; they ate together, prayed together, worshipped together, broke bread together, had fun together and it felt very much like church as it is meant to be.

Another couple, Andrew and Julia, joined the church in 2007 having heard about us through a mutual friend, and were attracted in particular by the vision to be a missionary

---

[113] www.hopetogether.org.uk (accessed 27th January 2021).

congregation in a rural setting. At that time they were very active in their local free evangelical church in Essex, and Andrew served on the eldership. One Sunday, they visited our church with their children, Hannah and Ben, stayed for lunch and sensed the call of God to move and be part of what God was doing here. The Lord has this wonderful habit of moving His people around to be in the right place at the right time. Andrew and Julia began to seek the Father's heart for a place to start a missional community. They began by prayer walking some of the new-build estates in surrounding villages and market towns.

They began to develop a vision for reaching people on one of these estates and began to gather a team, including some of our church members who lived there. It's an estate that is notionally part of a village community but is separated from its heart, including the church and primary school, by a busy main road, which in turn more directly connects it to a nearby market town. This separation is illustrated by the fact that some of the primary school-aged children attend the village school, while others commute to the one in the town.

The team first channelled their efforts into prayer and listening to the needs of the community. The next step was a simple one. Andrew and our son, Simon, went with a rugby ball to a green space on the estate and began kicking the ball to one another, and this attracted some teenage boys to join in. Snacks, cake and squash were provided, with craft activities added. Soon a mixed group of girls and boys came along. From the beginning there was always a five- to ten-minute slot for teaching from the Bible and prayer. This developed into a fuller twenty minutes, which might include worship, Bible teaching and prayer, backed up by Julia and Andrew visiting homes on the estate.

From the early days, the team struck up a positive link with the Residents' Association, which led us to our 'people of peace'. The Residents' Association had a passion to develop community on the estate, and there was therefore a sense of shared interest and purpose.

There is something of a seasonal monastic rhythm to this missional community. The only sheltered public place to meet on the estate is a portacabin, which limits the number who can get together. The main thrust of our activity has therefore been during the April to September period when we can gather more people by using an area of green space and erecting awnings to give a temporary covering.

During the summer period this missional community has met fortnightly, and by the summer of 2019 we were gathering up to forty young people for crafts, activities, football, refreshments – and always some form of God-thought delivered by a member of the team. This was backed up by some midweek activities throughout the year, including Glamgirls, reaching some of the younger teenage girls on the estate who may often be experiencing problems at home, school and socially. Just before Christmas 2019, the Glamgirls team organised (and paid for) the girls to have an outing to McDonald's. The team had asked the church to provide cosmetic and beauty products which could then be given to the girls as Christmas presents. The church responded in a typically generous fashion, and at the end of the meal each girl was presented with a bag full of goodies as a gift to take away with her. Of course, the gifts were given for their own sake, but hopefully they would also point to the generosity of God in giving the gift of Jesus. We hope and pray that the Glamgirls will find their identity and purpose as children of God deeply embraced and loved by the Father.

Andrew, Julia and the team greatly value the links with the Fountain of Life. One important aspect has been the connection with Kidz Klub. Pre-Covid, during the winter months when there was no meeting place on the estate, children were transported by bus to the monthly Fountain of Life Kidz Klub. The team also put on a weekend of mission at the end of each summer with a view to reaching families. These typically attracted up to 100 people from the estate, and it has been great to have the wider family of the Fountain of Life to draw from for the extra team needed for all of these various activities.

After we had worked with the people on the estate for a couple of years, we were somewhat taken aback to read in the local community magazine an advert for the estate's 'Community Church'. When Andrew asked the Residents' Association about it, the (then) chair explained, 'That's the name we've given you. You're our church.' It occurs to me that maybe we are hunting around for different vocabulary to describe what we do because we have lost confidence in the word 'church' more than the community around us has. When that community sees our faith applied in an authentic way, when they see our love as Christians for others worked out in practice, then perhaps the only vocabulary they have to describe what they see is, 'Here's the local church in action.' Truly the local church is the hope of the nation.

Julia talks about the twin track of falling in love with Jesus and falling in love with a people group. When we love people with our life, it shows. As Paul writes in his first letter to the Thessalonians, 'Because we loved you so much, we were delighted to share with you not only the gospel of God but our lives as well' (1 Thessalonians 2:8). Julia and Andrew and the rest of the team model this so well.

There is a plan for a new community centre to be built on the estate and Julia has been invited to sit on the planning committee for its furbishment and subsequent usage. The Residents' Association are keen that space is allocated to us for the continued work among families. It was even suggested that the team lead a service of dedication and celebration as part of the opening ceremony for the new building. We are not sure how this story will end, but the gates seem to have swung wide open. Let us see what God will do.

In October 2015, Angela and Tom were leading a missional community aimed at children in the village of Shouldham set in the adjacent Anglican diocese of Ely. It built on the work of a local mum who had set up a group in the local school aimed at reaching children. The founder of the group had moved away and Angela had a vision for taking it on and developing it further. Angela is a very creative person and introduced imaginative craft activities, drama, multimedia presentations and Bible story-telling. Then Angela and Tom heard about our church and the vision for missional communities. As they read our website, they recognised language which they felt described the heart of their vision. They decided to connect this group to the Fountain of Life because they felt it would give them a place of encouragement and accountability as well as access to resources, such as people and equipment. The churchwardens of their local church were very supportive of the work and welcomed it, but were not able to help in a practical way. The diocesan Fresh Expressions officer was also pleased that this provided a good structure that rooted the work and its leadership in an empowering community.

The missional community was named The Fountain at Shouldham, and there was a shift in emphasis from children to reaching whole families and the community. The focus was particularly on seeking to reach families who do not already belong to a church community. They cast their nets upon the waters[114] in many diverse ways. They held various 'gathering' events on Sunday mornings such as beach picnics, Pizza Church, Messy Church, Breakfast Church and Forest Church. Sometimes they organised all-age services at the local church school. They have hosted Alpha in a local pub and have run a small discipleship group in their home. They estimate that they are in regular contact with around fifty people.

As it developed and grew, the missional community attracted people from outside the immediate village and so it has been renamed The Fountain West Norfolk. Finding ways of keeping in contact with everyone across the network of relationships is a challenge. Angela is constantly looking for ways of connecting

---

[114] Saying drawn from the many allusions to fishing in the Gospels (for example, Matthew 4:19; John 21:6).

and building community. She set up a WhatsApp group which enabled her to build community and share Scripture, testimony, prayer requests and other encouragements.

There are challenges of discipleship and commitment: God becoming more than just 'an extra thing' in the lives of members, prioritising gatherings over other legitimate needs, discipling in Word and Spirit, equipping new members to strengthen the existing team and praying together as a group. But Angela has built a real and authentic community which is growing and bearing fruit.[115]

We have practised a 'low on control; high on accountability'[116] model. It is therefore vital that the lay leaders of these communities are supported, mentored and encouraged. We established an 'Apollos'[117] group as a means of supporting missional community leaders. Our practice has been to meet together at least quarterly to pray together, learn from one another, share experience and remind one another of our key values. This has built a strong relational bond between the leaders, which spills over between meetings and creates a culture of support and encouragement.

One couple who joined this group were from a church about thirty miles away from us and they connected with us for support. They have been involved in and led cell church and other missional activities and groups. In his role as community outreach worker, initially funded by Rural Ministries (RM) and

---

[115] All these local missional communities have contributed immensely in our response to Covid-19. They have delivered essential supplies and goodie bags, prayer walked their communities, organised outside services and online Alpha, provided craft activities, adventure trails and family activities. They have been a lifeline.

[116] For further information on this principle, see Hopkins and Breen, *Clusters: Creative Mid-Sized Missional Communities*, pp 39,141; see www.3dmovements.com (accessed 1st February 2021).

[117] Named after Apollos (Acts 18:24-28) who, after having been instructed by Priscilla and Aquila, was a 'great help to those who by grace had believed ... proving from the Scriptures that Jesus was the Messiah'.

the Laing Foundation,[118] Andy built a strong connection with the local care home, where he was involved in pastoral visiting and helping to lead regular services; he was keen to find ways of developing this into a place for a missional community. He was also involved with a church-based toddler group called Church Mice, and led an initiative to bring these two things together, taking the families from this group into the care home to meet some of the residents. Initially, children took in their toys and socialised with residents and, supported by their carers, involved them in their play. As time went on, one of the mums or the care home activity coordinator would prepare a simple craft which residents and children would sit round tables and do together. The time always ended with the singing of nursery rhymes, enjoyed by all, while Andy played the guitar. When Church Mice went through a quieter phase, Andy worked with the local reception teacher to take small groups of children in to share crafts and sing in a similar way. This continued as a regular activity until the first Covid-19 lockdown. Andy comments:

> It was wonderful to watch the way that residents 'came alive' through their interactions with the children, and to see the generations bond with much fun and laughter. Many of the children enjoyed the attention and interest shown, as they developed their natural social skills. Another advantage was that it brought the community into the care home, which can sometimes feel like an isolated place, building bridges with parents and carers too.

Other missional communities were formed around a particular age range or shared experience. Our Place was established to show the love of God to those who live with special needs and/or disabilities which sometimes make it difficult for members to find a place of acceptance and access to activities.

---

[118] See www.ruralministries.org.uk and www.laingfamilytrusts.org.uk (accessed 25th March 2021).

Church at 3 was introduced to be a monthly opportunity for families to gather, encounter God, develop faith and be discipled, with food, conversation, games and crafts, laced always with Bible teaching and worship for all ages together. Fun and light-hearted, Church at 3 provided a time when parents could encourage one another – an easy place to invite friends with young children to.

There were groups with a focus on those in their twenties and thirties and for those in their forties and fifties, and another formed around a shared interest and love for films and cinemagoing.

All this may seem a little fragmented, and it could so easily become so if all these activities were in isolation to each other. It is the community of the Fountain of Life that is the glue that has held all of them together, with the values and overall vision uniting us together as team.

They don't all work out. We had a photographic group formed around one man's vision which did not survive the leader moving away. Martin and Rosemarie had a vision for church in their community near Norwich. At the time, sensitivities concerning cross-parish boundaries hampered growth, so they continued to meet in their home. Then they were approached by the CEO of Rural Ministries who had heard of their vision for the community. He offered them the use of a building that was shortly due to become vacant. It used to be an old Methodist chapel. Martin and Rosemarie asked if it could come under our umbrella as a type of missional community. RM were looking for closer local accountability for Martin and Rosemarie, so it seemed a good way forward and an opportunity for us all to work together. It was a perfect partnership for us.

In 2011 we commissioned a core team of four, including Martin and Rosemarie, and a wider group of twelve to form a missional community called The Rock. Our team led worship at the opening event. They experienced life and growth, mainly owing to two significant ministries. The first of these was the

Rock Café that became so popular that Rosemarie comments, 'We had to decide whether to continue to put all our energies into building what was becoming a very successful "business", or use the café setting and facilities to serve the ministries we were running. We chose the latter.' The second significant ministry was that of totZrock which started out with a handful of children coming to The Rock Café with their mothers and grew to more than seventy mums registered. They met twice weekly with up to thirty children at each session. Rosemarie also organised many Messy Church events which were always well supported by the friends and families of the totZrock mums and children. It was a great success, but it proved hard to sustain. The main reason was that the core team never expanded and became exhausted. The most likely place to draw help from would have been the Fountain of Life, but as this was around forty-five minutes away, it was too far to provide regular support of team 'on the ground'.

Rosemarie became increasingly frustrated that the 'church' membership didn't grow. Sunday 'services' attracted Christians from other churches rather than making disciples of those connecting through totZrock and Messy Church. It needed someone else to be alongside Martin and Rosemarie to build on the excellent foundations that had been laid. Eventually, at Rosemarie's request, the decision was taken by RM to fund a full-time pastor to grow the church. However, funds to do this were not likely to be forthcoming for two years, if at all. So, despite everyone's best efforts and the undeniable fruitful engagement in mission, it came to an end.

Sometimes it is hard to know exactly what stops something flourishing. Probably a combination of the above factors. In the end the decision to close The Rock and its ministries was made. In Rosemarie's words, 'Reluctantly, we closed the doors on a thriving mother and toddler ministry which remains a sadness to this day.'

In one sense, it's OK. Missional communities can come and go as the Spirit leads. Others have and will stand the test of time, and some will become more fully church than others. It's the emerging work of the Holy Spirit as we engage with our communities that produces church. How He does it and who He does it with is His affair, and I'm happy to leave it that way.

Disappointments, though, do need to be handled well. In order for these initiatives to have the chance of life, they have to be named and spoken well of in the church as a whole. That means raising their profile. When things don't turn out as we had hoped, it is important to own it and make sure that people know we're still committed to the concept, even if one example of it has not worked as well as we might have hoped. It is also important to celebrate the life that has been lived, however short, and affirm those who carried the vision. Nothing is wasted in the kingdom.

It's always easier to lead with hindsight. My conviction that the Holy Spirit is at work in releasing what we have ended up calling 'missional community' has been validated in the fruit that so many have produced. But I have made many mistakes in pursuing the vision. I have used different language at times, often swayed by how others are communicating rather than by what the Spirit is saying to us, here, in our context, for our location. I have not communicated clearly enough or articulated the vision sharply or consistently enough at times. Things have not always worked out as I had anticipated or declared. Fortunately, the church I have led has been patient with me and allowed us to go on a journey together, without really knowing either the destination or quite how to get there. It's been challenging but exciting and fulfilling, especially for those who have ended up leading these communities.

It is an adventure. We are pioneering. Let's not 'despise the day of small things' (Zechariah 4:10), for God is always at work.

8
Engaging With the Word

'Is not my word like fire,' declares the LORD, 'and like
a hammer that breaks a rock in pieces?'
(Jeremiah 23:29)

'You're from Norfolk? You must meet Freddy and Ali. They have a vision for Norfolk.'

It was early January 2006. Pippa and I were having a week's retreat in the Peak District. It was our custom to start the year by creating space for us to spend time together as a couple, to enjoy time walking in the hills and to seek God for the year ahead.

On the Sunday morning, we decided to visit the Philadelphia Centre in Sheffield, a church that had been planted by the parish church, St Thomas Crookes. It was a church that in some ways shared our story, and one that had been helpful in our own development. We arrived early for the service, having misread the start time, and Freddy and Ali were there early too, having wrongly thought that they were on the welcoming team that week. The person on the door who had welcomed us made the introduction and we enjoyed a long chat over a coffee seated on comfortable, red sofas. At the time, Freddy worked in the ACPI offices as researcher and administrator for Bob and Mary Hopkins. In fact, I had spoken to Freddy the previous week while attempting to contact Bob to discuss Clusters and

Lifeshapes.[119] He had registered the word 'Norfolk' and noted the Clusters and Lifeshapes connection. He and Ali were therefore already praying about the Fountain of Life before we met on that Sunday morning, an early indicator of 'call'.[120]

By the end of our conversation, seeds had been sown, which were to germinate in an extraordinary way. It would prove to be a life-changing moment for Freddy and Ali, and highly significant for us as a church. At the time, we left Freddy and Ali excited and committed to visiting us to explore the conversation further. There were lots of connections. Ali's parents lived in Norfolk, and Freddy and Ali had served on the Beach Mission at Sheringham for several years. They had been thinking already about Norwich, but on the weekend before they met Pippa and me, a friend of theirs had shared with them a prophetic sense of seeing them positioned thirty miles west of Norwich. We are located slightly west of central Norfolk – about twenty-eight miles west of Norwich. It seemed close enough!

A couple of months later, Freddy and Ali travelled down to visit the church, and a year later, by then with Maisie, at the time a babe in arms, visited again – this time for Freddy to preach. A process of discernment began which, three years later, in 2009, culminated in them moving from Sheffield to Ashill. During this time they met with members of the staff team and our trustees and made an instant connection. There was a general sense of agreement that the Lord was calling them here and a great deal of excitement at what God would do through them. It was clear that they were moving not just to be part of the church but also to play a key part in shaping its future and that

---

[119] Lifeshapes is a course first developed by Mike Breen, then vicar at St Thomas Church, Crookes, Sheffield, and now known as 'A Passionate Life'. Mike Breen and Walt Kallestad, *A Passionate Life* (Colorado, CO: Cook Communications Ministries; Eastbourne: Kingsway Communications, 2005).

[120] For example, in the story of Peter and Cornelius in Acts 10.

in particular Freddy would be working alongside me in a strategic way.

Freddy and I thought we knew exactly what that would look like – Clusters and Lifeshapes. He and Ali had led a Cluster in Sheffield. As referred to in the previous chapter, Clusters were mid-sized groups that engaged with smaller communities outside the larger, gathered congregation that met in the church building. They had experienced leading one such group of about thirty. They had also participated in the Lifeshapes course which we had started to introduce at the Fountain, and so it was natural to imagine Freddy taking a lead in this. However, Freddy and Ali's attempts at starting a mid-sized community in a nearby market town didn't take off, and we stopped running Lifeshapes after a year. A salutary reminder that God's ways and thoughts are infinitely higher than ours (Isaiah 55:9), for God was about to open new doors for us all.

The move had been a huge step of faith for Freddy and Ali, who left jobs, house and friends behind in Sheffield to effectively start again. Almost immediately upon arrival, an amazing job opportunity came for Ali, which matched perfectly her specialist scientific background. Freddy had become self-employed a couple of months before moving, as a writer, editor, speaker and publisher. His main work was writing for ACPI and writing and editing for Fresh Expressions, but his work did also take in other teaching, writing and publishing projects.

The whole family settled well into the Fountain and quickly became established as part of the family. But it was Freddy's career in particular that began to develop and grow and impact the Fountain of Life.

Freddy's background before joining ACPI was as a secondary school teacher and we quickly discovered that he had a sharp intellect and substantial Bible knowledge and possessed excellent teaching and communication skills. Freddy came with a fair amount of experience of preaching at mid-sized community level and, outside church meetings, had been a speaker at several events focused on Clusters, mission and church planting. He had also just moved on from editing the Mission-Shaped Ministry course to being one of its primary writers, often focusing mainly on the theological side of things. But, as Freddy observes:

> None of it equated to a main focus on teaching/ preaching or identifying as a theologian – everything I did served a broader perspective in apostolic pioneering – and it was certainly Fountain of Life that fully recognised it, much more than I did, and really invested in me moving from the fringes of ministries to stepping into my own.

Looking back, from the Fountain's perspective, all of this was getting everything into place to further develop our ability to disciple people through their understanding and application of the Scriptures. This was an aspect of our life together in which we wanted to grow, and Freddy was clearly part of God's plan for how this would be shaped moving forward, as we shall discover later in this chapter.

I remember, shortly after moving to Norfolk, attending a Spring Harvest[121] seminar entitled 'Uncaging the Lion'. The focus of this was on exploring tools that would enable every believer to meet with God through His Word, helping them to go deeper in their understanding and discover new truths for themselves. This principle, together with our own personal experience of being discipled through the Scriptures, probably laid a core foundation in me of the need to equip every member of the body to be able to hear God for themselves through the Word. This requires us to be able to read Scripture contextually, understand how the Bible fits together, be able to find Jesus in the Old Testament as well as the New, and encounter the God of the Bible afresh in our culture and situation today.

---

[121] An annual Christian event, see www.springharvest.org (accessed 26th March 2021).

We already prioritised the teaching and preaching ministry, having a high expectation that lives would be changed as a result. In our preparation, therefore, we would always seek to ask two questions: What does God want His people to know? What response or application does God want us to make to that knowledge? Sometimes we would give people little 'takeaways' which have included bookmarks, carved wooden donkeys and wooden hearts inscribed with verses to remind them of the teaching point during the week.

As an Anglican church, we have the great advantage of following the Lectionary[122] which, over a three-year period, sets out the recommended passages to be read on any given day. Usually, we have allowed this to govern our Bible readings Sunday by Sunday. One of these is usually a psalm, and we have become used to joining in as a congregation in reading the appointed one for that day. It is often in reading the Psalms that we find words to express our praise and worship, as well as our emotional response to the events of life. Following the Lectionary ensured that we stretched the comfort zone of those who preached. We couldn't settle in the furrows of our favourite topics or passages, but were confronted with sitting under the authority of God's Word and allowing it to set the theme. The Sunday before Covid-19 broke, we were treated to a sermon on death, which proved exceptionally timely. Without the discipline of the Lectionary, it would be easy to avoid these more difficult subjects.

In 2005, we had introduced an evening service called 'Feed the Soul' which had the aim of preaching expositionally through the whole Bible. Term by term we worked our way through all the books of the Bible, one or two chapters at a time. It was a service aimed at believers and attended by members of other churches as well as our own members. Fifteen years later we completed the journey!

---

[122] www.chpublishing.co.uk/features/lectionary (accessed 27th January 2021).

Perhaps we are sometimes guilty of placing a higher value on preaching and teaching than on the Scriptures themselves having power of their own to speak. We need to understand the original context and apply it to today's, but as the American pastor and author Timothy Keller puts it, 'Preaching biblically … means preaching the Word and not your opinion. When we preach the Scriptures we are speaking "the very words of God" (1 Peter 4:11).'[123] The Bible has a high view of itself. It is like a 'double-edged sword' (Hebrews 4:12), it never returns empty (Isaiah 55:11), it is like a hammer capable of smashing the hardest of rock (Jeremiah 23:29), it is like a seed that germinates and produces life (Matthew 13:23), it is 'useful for teaching, rebuking, correcting and training in righteousness'. What gives the Word its authority over us? It is both its nature and its source. It is, after all, 'God-breathed' (2 Timothy 3:16). Simply hearing Scripture breaks open hearts.

Recently someone called the office and said, 'I don't go to church but I think I should start reading the Bible. Where should I begin?' A sign of the openness of our culture right now to God and a great encouragement that reading the Bible is still in date! So, let's have confidence in the Word to simply speak for itself.

Our interns took this seriously when they organised a continuous read through the whole Bible. I forget quite how many hours it took (David Suchet took around eighty hours[124]), but it was read through the day and night, culminating in time for the main Sunday morning service.

Over the years we have provided daily Bible reading notes, working our way through the Bible in various ways: we have used three- and five-year plans, sometimes organised in chronological order, or alternating between the Old and New Testaments to give variety. These notes used to be written by

[123] Timothy Keller, *Preaching* (London: Hodder & Stoughton, 2015), p20.
[124] Holy Bible (NIV) read by David Suchet, www.hodderbibles.co.uk (accessed 20th October 2020).

the church leader, but we began to look for people within the congregation who we felt had the potential to be contributors. Each person would be asked to write notes for three consecutive days. The notes were limited to 450 words in length and supported by a prayer or thought to conclude. They were, of course, subject to being edited to give an overall consistency, but over the years a team of around forty has been released to contribute. A significant multiplication from the model of the 'one' leader contributing them all.

All of this built up the biblical literacy of the body of Christ. We were putting in little building blocks that exposed people to the power of God's Word and developed their ability to communicate that to others.

Jane's story is an illustration. I asked her to contribute some Bible readings. This opportunity gave Jane the incentive of writing to a deadline and contributed to her sense of this being something that God wanted her to develop further. Her writing and broadcasting career has since developed, including writing an excellent book based on her personal experience of miscarriage, which has been helpful to many in dealing with this in their own lives or wanting to be a support to others experiencing loss in this way.[125] Another story illustrating how God can do so much more than we could 'ask or imagine' (Ephesians 3:20) when we give Him something to work with and allow Him to develop our gifts and ministries.

We wanted to do more in equipping lay leaders in our church theologically. Especially as a church known for its 'charismatic' emphasis, I considered it important to place a high value on holding a rigorous attitude to Scripture, allowing it to inform and establish our practice. Alpha was a great starting point for all – one that most incomers to the church had been through. We had added courses looking at key doctrines, addressing

---

[125] Jane Clamp, *Too Soon: A Mother's Journey Through Miscarriage* (London: SPCK, 2018).

ethical issues, exploring mission praxis and building a kingdom lifestyle. All of this whetted the appetite for more.

In 2011, along came WTC (Westminster Theological Centre). WTC was at the time led by Crispin Fletcher-Louis, whose vision was to deliver kingdom theology courses in partnership with local 'hub' churches.[126] These programmes of theological training would be delivered locally, supported nationally and accredited by a recognised university. This seemed to be the answer for us, fulfilling our desire to equip leaders with a sound theological perspective, and biblical confidence in our charismatic understanding of life in the Spirit. It also proved to be the missing piece in the jigsaw of God's plan for Freddy. We needed someone to pioneer and then run the local hub. I approached Freddy and he agreed to be our first hub director. The church embraced it and gave £25,000 to cover the start-up costs, students were recruited and the East Anglian hub was born. Being in such a rural area was always a challenge but it is precisely in this rather more isolated, and often overlooked, context of rural ministry that we need access to high-quality biblical training, support and development.

Our intake of new students varied from four to eight each year, each one travelling up to two hours for our Tuesday hub nights. Over the years, we have had some wonderful testimonies of the impact that studying with WTC has had on individuals. Here are some of them.

Matt Beckett spent a year studying with WTC to satisfy his

> desire to deepen my theological understanding and skills. But what I found was that the heart of learning with WTC was more than just a desire to increase the head knowledge of the participants. Instead, their model created a worshipping community that sought to put into practice, in our own lives, the biblical truths discovered as we dug deeper into each text.

---

[126] wtctheology.org.uk (accessed 27th January 2021).

Randall had moved from the outskirts of London to the middle of Norfolk and had been praying that the Lord would lead him to the right theology course, and,

> as only God can, he led me to a church that was directly connected to possibly the most perfect theology course for me at WTC. I did a postgraduate diploma in Kingdom Theology. The course was academically very challenging but also life-changing as it gave me exposure to some of the best theological minds around, from the UK, the USA and Canada. Certain parts of the Bible suddenly had a new meaning and a greater clarity. It was as if my faith had been given a deeper foundation. For me, as a pragmatic, rational, though Spirit-filled Christian, it gave my belief a legitimacy and context. I could clearly see what my faith was all about and what my purpose was, and that was 'to facilitate bringing in the kingdom of God'.

Michael found studying with WTC transformative:

> I remember Crispin, then one of the founders, speaking at a New Wine seminar about it, saying that the intention wasn't to teach students what to think, but to give them 'a grid' for understanding the Bible. I found that it did exactly that, which means I now have a lifelong tool for helping me to encounter God through Bible study. I also think I was profoundly blessed to have such a resource, literally on my doorstep at the very time I was actively considering doing something like that.

In due time Michael succeeded Freddy as our hub director: 'It was my privilege to help pass on that blessing to others, and I was and continue to be encouraged by the students who studied during my tenure there. I suspect the legacy of those WTC years will be long-lasting.'

Shortly after we set out on the WTC journey, Freddy and I had a conversation about his own development. It was very clear that there was a calling upon his life in teaching and preaching. We recognised a particular anointing upon him to communicate God's Word in a way that produced significant and lasting fruit. With his role as hub director, he was connected to the world of academia and if he was to prosper further, then he needed to increase his academic qualifications. With WTC on our doorstep, this was an opportunity for him to seize and I encouraged him to study towards an MA in Theology with them. There were two obstacles: time and money. Freddy's parents said to him, 'If you can find the time, we'll pay your fees.' The next day Freddy received an email from me which said, 'If you can find the fees, we'll cover the cost of your time.' God was making a way. Doing this course confirmed a strong sense in Freddy that academia was a life-giving environment for him, and one that sharpened his ongoing teaching ministry in the church.[127]

Having the WTC hub, significant as it was, did not meet our desire to develop everyone's ability to engage more deeply with God's Word. It was a big personal commitment to sign up for theological training of this nature. At the time, the cost was close to £2,000 per annum and it could take as many as six years for someone to gain a full degree. There were options, of course, to do shorter courses, but even a certificate would take two years to gain. It was not just the financial cost. People needed to be able to make the time available too. So we needed something else: something that though unaccredited would be similarly relevant, in-depth and stretching – but much more accessible for everyone. So we developed 'Digging Deeper', an open access course in biblical studies and theology. I say 'we': the content and syllabus was pretty much developed by Freddy and he for the most part led the course.

---

[127] Freddy has recently been appointed as director of Undergraduate Studies at WTC.

The format of Digging Deeper was unlike anything we had ever run before. Most of our church teaching was delivered in a didactic way with the preacher expositing truth, hopefully in a way that led to application, but the focus was on the delivery and the deliverer. By contrast, Freddy modelled a conversational teaching style that enabled those on the course to reach conclusions for themselves. He encouraged the raising of difficult questions, questions that perhaps people had been afraid to ask, and encouraged them to dig deeper into the Scriptures, to trace how understanding of God and His ways develops through Scripture. It was much more of an interactive style laced with teaching input from Freddy or whoever was leading the session. We developed this course and ran it for several years both at Ashill and Norwich to great effect. We found this influenced the life of our home groups, as people who had attended Digging Deeper took back what they had learned to their groups. Eventually a lay leadership team emerged for Digging Deeper which spread the load and enabled others to develop their teaching gifts.

Kerri found Digging Deeper amazing:

> I felt closer to God as I felt I was getting to understand His words and His message to us more. It helped me to really 'dig in' to the Bible and helped me to understand it better, especially the Old Testament. It made me question things, and the environment felt safe so you did not feel stupid when you asked something. It was so valuable hearing other people's views of the passages we were studying. The teaching was of such a high standard and it was wonderful to have that opportunity to study at that level.

On later courses Freddy asked Kerri to lead some sessions. She reflected on her experience of this: 'Personally it helped me grow and step out in faith as I was able to help facilitate some of the sessions, which then rolled into me being able to step up in front of church.'

Rachel, who was a student from its beginning, comments:

> I found it to be a deeply enriching experience; in fact, I
> would go so far as to say, life-changing.
>
> Exploring the beautiful and abundant gift of the
> Word, guided by a brilliant and passionate Bible teacher,
> surrounded by loving and discerning fellow diggers,
> helped me better understand biblical truths and
> challenged my preconceived ideas.
>
> I had many experiences of the Holy Spirit speaking
> through others or directly to me with exciting revelations
> and nuggets of truth to be discussed then and there or for
> deeper exploration on my own later. It felt as though
> Jesus Himself was sitting among us in our discussions,
> which of course He was, in and through each one of us,
> living and speaking and teaching.
>
> I have been challenged, convicted, encouraged,
> inspired, empowered and blessed!

We seek to be a people who are discipled by the Word. The
Bible is complex – there are passages that are difficult to
interpret and understand, apparent discrepancies and
inconsistencies, but God has spoken through His Word,
through the law, the prophets and, of course, most supremely
through His Son (Hebrews 1:2). In the Scriptures we find God's
general plan and purposes for how we relate to Him, how we
relate to others and how we find our place in the world around
us. We seek to allow His Word to shape us and form us, which
means allowing it to have an authority over our lives. In this way
the Word of God becomes what it is intended to be – 'the sword
of the Spirit' (Ephesians 6:17).

Perhaps the greatest contemporary challenge to us in sitting
under the authority of the Word of God is our attitude to issues
of sexuality. There were increasingly times when I was asked
about this and I felt it was important that we had something in
writing to which we could direct people. I was also of the view
that, in forming a response, it is hard to avoid our theological

or biblical perspective being unduly influenced by our own personal and pastoral experience, or our desire to be a relevant voice in the culture. We needed to be clear about our doctrine, but pastorally sensitive and grace-filled in the way we applied it. I rather like Gavin Calver's (chief executive of Evangelical Alliance) call for the Church to be 'braver and kinder'.[128] Sexuality is one of those areas where I believe this to be so true. So I set out to write a policy document that would seek to articulate our doctrinal and pastoral position. Doctrinal, because we aimed to be consistent with an orthodox biblical perspective. Pastoral, because we recognised that our culture is set at a distance from this. In it we set out our vision, and I quote from it:

> Our aim is to raise a generation who are committed to pursuing a lifestyle of sexual purity consistent with Biblical teaching. We want to hold out hope to our broken and disordered world by affirming that the Bible's teaching on sex, marriage and singleness is good news whether our vocation is to be married or single.
>
> We believe that our sexuality is intended to be physically expressed solely within the context of marriage as a covenant of love between one man and one woman. All other forms of sexual practice fall short of this ideal, are less than God made us for and do not therefore represent His best for us or the society of which we are a part.
>
> We recognise that we live in a culture with very mixed experiences and expectations in this sphere of sexual ethics. We are called to engage with that often broken and disordered culture, challenge it and be incarnate within it in order to hold out the hope of Jesus and the power of restorative love. We are committed to modelling a positive vision of the family of God as an inclusive place

---

[128] www.eauk.org/about-us/giving/appeals/braver-kinder-2020-1 (accessed 27th January 2021).

of belonging in which all, irrespective of sexual orientation, may find the possibility of a vibrant and fulfilling life in fellowship with Christ and one another.

I went on to explore the values that followed from this, and the pastoral implications. We discussed it at our staff and trustees meetings. Not everyone agreed with it all, but there was an appreciation that it sought to hold together truth and grace as being at the heart of our response.

Often it is not 'what' but 'how we put things' that creates animosity. A friend of mine preached on human sexuality and was approached by a couple afterwards who were in a civil same-sex partnership at the time. They thanked him for his sermon, which surprised him.

He said, 'I thought that you would have been hating every word of it.'

They replied that they disagreed with everything but loved the way he said it.

It is possible to disagree well, but people need to be led and they need to know not just what the leader thinks but also the scriptural basis for their interpretation.

Our culture does fall short, as do our own lives, but that should not deter us from holding out the hope of a better way. I have found Glynn Harrison's book *A Better Story* so helpful in looking at these particular issues. I could include many quotes, but let this one suffice:

> Let's acknowledge the scale of the challenge before us. In today's world the revival of a confident, biblically rooted vision of human flourishing in the sphere of sex and relationships looks like a pipe dream. Our culture seems so far adrift of its Christian foundations that it is almost impossible to imagine it. But imagine it we must. As I write in the shadow of Good Friday, I'm reminded that nothing looked more impossible than that Jesus would rise from the dead. Believers have been here before. Countless numbers paid the price for what they believed

in, some with their lives. If we truly believe that what we have been given is life for the world, it is our turn now to stand up and be counted.[129]

It ought to be possible for us to contend for an orthodox position that views marriage as a lifelong commitment between a man and a woman, a sacrament that is holy in God's eyes. Further, to foster and contend for an understanding that individuals, families and society as a whole are all much more likely to flourish when sexual activity is preserved within this boundary. We don't, however, pastor within a holy enclosure. Vicars can no longer (if they ever did) impose a lifestyle from on high. But there are things we can do. We as leaders can seek to model well celibacy or marriage, according to the state of our calling. We can seek to create church communities that embrace singles as well as the marrieds. We can choose to walk in the example of Jesus and reach out to those who are not yet pursuing the ideal. We can walk with those who struggle with issues of sexual identity. We must be prepared to fail and be misunderstood. Church is family, and if it is, then we have a responsibility to treat people as if they were our very own children. If one of our own children were to behave in a way that contradicted a core belief, then surely we would still love them and include them in the family.

As a church we include those who have differing views on this issue. It speaks louder than words about the seriousness of our desire to be a family to which all can belong. But what happens when those in a practising same-sex relationship want to get more involved within the church? I don't have all the answers. I think I know where I would draw the line but I don't believe there is a one-size-fits-all response to complex discipleship issues. We have to be led by the Spirit and that can mean handling one situation differently from another. It can get us into trouble because we can be accused of inconsistency or

[129] Glynn Harrison, *A Better Story: God, Sex & Human Flourishing* (London: IVP, 2017), pxix.

preferment. My own rule of thumb is to place a greater emphasis on the convicting power of the Holy Spirit than the wisdom of the vicar! It can lead to transformation.

Here's an example drawn from a different context. Jack attended an Alpha course with his wife, June, and 'realised what was missing in my life, Jesus, and I wanted to come into the warmth and light that He sheds'.[130] Two years later, he attended a weekend conference at the Fountain and one of the speakers spoke about the dangers of Freemasonry. Jack was still a practising Freemason and did not see any conflict between that and his new-found faith. In the days following the conference, Jack became increasingly incensed by

> what I considered to be the total injustice of his ranting [and] I eventually took my concerns to Stephen who listened to my problem and sent me away with a book written by Ian Gordon, which explained why Freemasonry and a true Christian are not compatible.[131] I came to realise that my Masonic beliefs did not include Jesus and in certain ceremonies I was uttering blasphemies.

It was undoubtedly the convicting power of the Holy Spirit coming upon Jack that led to this particular moment when he could move forward in this area of his life. He resigned from all Masonic membership, destroyed his regalia and Masonic Bible and renounced his previous involvement. He described himself as now 'at peace and a more complete person'.

It is the work of the Spirit to apply God's Word to our hearts in a way that divides 'soul and spirit, joints and marrow' (Hebrews 4:12). It is to the ongoing discipling work of the Spirit that we must now turn our attention.

---

[130] Based on the written testimony of Jack given to the author in 2014.
[131] Ian Gordon, *The Craft and the Cross* (Kirby Bedon: The Branch Press, 1989).

9
Discipled by the Spirit

'Not by might nor by power, but by my Spirit,' says the
LORD.
(Zechariah 4:6)

Billy and Vicky and their three children came to church one
Sunday morning. They had been invited to come along in
celebration of Dick and Eileen's golden wedding anniversary.
They had been invited to come to church many times before.
They saw this as the opportunity to do so and put a stop to all
those invitations!

It was Billy's first experience of church for a while; his
previous experience of church and Christians had not been
great. Here, he felt very welcomed and not judged. During the
coffee break, people he had never met before started coming up
and talking to him. They seemed genuinely interested in his life.
During the time of singing, as he looked at those around him, it
was clear that people were expressing their faith in a way that
was personal and intimate. They were not singing *about* God but
to Him. There was real relationship. There was a joy and a
confidence and trust about their expression of 'worship' that
moved him. He enjoyed the service, but it was in itself
unremarkable until the blessing was given at the end and the
Holy Spirit was invited to come. He describes it as being 'like
having a warm shower', and he heard God say to him, 'You've

been messing around for thirty-six years, now it's time to follow Me.' He felt a peace and joy that he had never experienced before. It was all very gentle, and no one around Billy, least of all his wife, was particularly aware at the time of what was happening to him. This was his first experience of encountering the immanent presence of God – of knowing that he was loved by the creator of the universe.

Billy went home with his wife and three young children a changed person. So much so that over lunch, Vicky turned to him and said, 'What has happened to you? It's like you're a different man.' Billy had some explaining to do, and the problem was that he didn't really fully understand what had just happened. No surprise, then, to see them all back in church the following Sunday, and they joined one of our midweek home groups.

Then they began to experience spiritual opposition. For a few weeks, every time they attempted to set off for church or home group, one or other of their children would suddenly become sick, until Vicky's mum came round, prayed in the house and the sickness stopped.

Vicky began to dislike the fact that Billy was a Christian, but people were praying for her, and after a few months Vicky finally surrendered her life to God and welcomed Jesus into her life in a fresh way. The following year, amid much celebration, they were both baptised by full immersion.

Their baptism was in 2012. Since then life has been far from easy for them as a family. Vicky has suffered from serious depression at times, two of their children have had significant ill-health, they have experienced job losses and financial challenges. For many years Billy continued to wrestle with chronic fatigue syndrome (CFS/ME). At our Father's Heart Weekend in 2016, a member of the visiting Catch the Fire[132] team prayed for him and since then his chronic fatigue has gone.

[132] Catch the Fire is an international family of churches and ministries. See www.ctflondon.com (accessed 23rd February 2021).

More recently, Billy was diagnosed with prostate cancer, and was operated on to remove his prostate with the hope that this would remove the cancer. The cancer, however, had already spread to his lymph nodes and other parts of his body. He still has cancer but at the present time it is dormant. An uncertain future. But Billy has a peace about it all, 'knowing that God has got it. I don't know what the big plan is because I can only see the little picture. God sees the bigger one. I may be in a raging storm but Jesus is still asleep in the back of the boat[133] so it can't be that bad.' In the midst of his suffering, still Billy chooses to worship the God who loves him. An inspiring story of faith.

The Holy Spirit is the stealth weapon of the Church. One of our core values is to be discipled by the Spirit as well as by the Word. Therefore when we meet together we seek to create space for God to move by the power of the Spirit, giving people opportunity to be filled with the Holy Spirit.

In the New Testament there are different ways of speaking about the activity of the Spirit. There's 'baptism in the Spirit', which Jesus Himself experiences when the Spirit comes upon Him and He hears the affirming words of the Father: 'You are my Son, whom I love; with you I am well pleased' (Luke 3:22). In Ephesians Paul uses the language of being 'filled with the Spirit' (Ephesians 5:18) – words expressed in the present imperative emphasising the requirement to 'be filled' continuously. Baptism suggests that there is always a first time of experiencing the fullness of the Spirit, whereas being filled suggests that there is always more. We could paraphrase D L Moody and, if asked, 'Have you been filled with the Spirit?' respond with, 'Yes, but I leak.'[134] There is always more for us to receive.

Sometimes the Scriptures emphasise the role of the Spirit in us to shape us and form us (eg John 14:17; 2 Corinthians 3:18);

---

[133] A reference to Mark 4:38.

[134] American evangelist in the nineteenth century; his actual words were 'I need a continual infilling because I leak', www.family-times.net/illustration/Blessing/201911 (accessed 28th January 2021).

at other times the Scriptures speak about the Spirit being upon us to anoint and equip us (Luke 24:49; Acts 1:8). The Spirit is in us to bend us into His likeness and upon us to send us out into the world. He is in us for our sake, to grow us into His likeness, and upon us to reflect His image to those around us. We perhaps should be careful not to draw too fine a distinction, but it is helpful to have these two dimensions in mind when considering what it means to be filled with the Spirit.

One of the images presented by the apostle Paul for us as individuals and corporately as the Church is that of the temple of God (1 Corinthians 3:16; 2 Corinthians 6:16). In the Old Testament the temple was the physical place identified as housing or hosting the presence of God (2 Chronicles 5:14). One of the complaints of the exiled people of God was, 'Where can I go to meet with God' now that the temple had been destroyed and they were in a foreign land (Psalm 137:1-4)? Yet it was precisely in this place of exile that the prophet Ezekiel experienced the presence of God, far removed from Jerusalem and the temple building (Ezekiel 1:1). He went on to speak of an even greater day when God would 'put [His] Spirit in you and move you to follow [His] decrees and be careful to keep [His] laws' (Ezekiel 36:27). A promise that gave the 'how' to the promise given by God to Jeremiah: 'I will put my law in their minds and write it on their hearts. I will be their God, and they will be my people ... they will all know me' (Jeremiah 31:33-34). Later, Joel would look ahead to a day when God would 'pour out [His] Spirit on all people' (Joel 2:28). On the day of Pentecost Peter turned to this promise to explain the events of that day (Acts 2:17-21).

I love the vision given to Ezekiel of a river flowing out of the temple towards the Dead Sea. As it flows, new life follows. Even the waters of the Dead Sea become fresh and full of living creatures. Wherever the river flows there are large numbers of fish, fruit trees of all kinds with permanent fruit and foliage which provide food and healing (Ezekiel 47:1-12).

When Jesus spoke in the temple at the Feast of Tabernacles, He pointed to Himself as the new temple when He declared, 'Whoever believes in me, as Scripture has said, rivers of living water will flow from within them' (John 7:38). Jesus promises this living water to the woman at the well (John 4:14), and her response transforms a community. In that moment she becomes a temple on legs, taking the presence of God to her town, and the living water flows through her so people come to know that 'this man really is the Saviour of the world' (John 4:42).

This is not just a nice idea. It's a reality into which we are invited. We get to have the extraordinary honour and privilege of hosting the presence of God. It changes our lives, but is never intended to stop with us. It is intended to flow and transform others and even whole communities. It is only as we are renewed in the power of the Spirit that we can be His ambassadors (2 Corinthians 5:20), His representatives to the world around us.

There is no abundance of money or clever strategy that can change the nation. There is no other way for the Church to be renewed than by the power of the Spirit. All it needs is followers who are willing to pray and be radically open to receiving the fullness of the Spirit. I love the story of Peter and John in Acts 4 when they are being held to account before the Sanhedrin for having healed the crippled man at the temple. When those in charge saw their courage and 'realised that they were unschooled, ordinary men, they were astonished and they took note that these men had been with Jesus' (Acts 4:13).

This is at the heart of our story. It's at the heart of my story too. Back in 1981, when I became a Christian, I attended my first Alpha course, which included a weekend teaching on the Holy Spirit. A group of about thirty of us went away for the weekend, and during this there was an opportunity to ask to be filled with the Spirit. I stood with my hands outstretched and eyes closed, not entirely sure what to expect. I remember it being during the half-time interval of a football match that we were playing! As far as I was aware, nothing at all happened, and I went back to playing football apparently unmoved.

A few months later, the church I attended was visited by John Wimber[135] and I went along to some teaching sessions on the Spirit. I remember at the end of one of these sessions he prayed for the Spirit to come, and I stood once again with my arms outstretched and eyes firmly closed. As he and his team prayed, I felt a heaviness and found myself needing to sit down. I was not particularly aware of the passing of time, but it transpired that I was one of the last to leave the meeting. I was very aware of experiencing a deep sense of peace, calmness and contentment which is hard to put into words, but it all helped me understand in a fresh way the words of Jesus spoken to His disciples when He breathed His Spirit upon them: 'Peace be with you!' (John 20:19).

Since then, I have been prayed with on innumerable occasions to be filled with the Spirit. Sometimes I have been aware of God at work at the time, but mostly not. My experience would be that God knows when I need to hear from Him, or to be particularly aware of His presence.

One particular occasion that was a significant 'life' experience happened at Toronto Airport Vineyard in 1995. As I was being prayed for I had a vision of myself playing on a beach. The tide then went out to the far horizon and I followed it until the seabed became dry and cracked. At that point a huge tidal wave came and engulfed me. I felt no fear at the time, although as a young child living near Blackpool I remember a recurring nightmare of being swept off the beach by a tidal wave! The scene then switched back to me playing on the beach. I sensed the words 'Perfect love casts out fear'[136] and a promise from the Father that He would always satisfy my thirst.

---

[135] At the time John Wimber was pastor of the Vineyard Anaheim, California, and subsequently led the Vineyard Movement; see www.vineyardanaheim.com for current information on the Anaheim Vineyard.

[136] 1 John 4:18, NKJV. NIV has: 'perfect love drives out fear'.

Let me make four observations before we move on. First, please know that being filled with the Spirit is not necessarily something that we experience in a tangible or conscious way. We are called to receive by faith and faith is described as having 'confidence in what we hope for and assurance about what we do not see' (Hebrews 11:1) or feel. Second, be aware that most physical manifestations of the Spirit at work in us are our reaction or response as a frail human being to the power of God at work. Third, being filled with the Spirit is a surrender of self-control which remains wholly voluntary. We allow the Holy Spirit to come and take control. At any time we can choose to stop the Spirit ministering to us. The ministry of the Spirit involves a continuous cooperation between Him and me. Finally, even though when we are open to the Spirit in this way, we may not notice anything different about ourselves, others around us usually do. It might be to do with our values and priorities, the way we speak, our character, our countenance or even physical attributes. On one Alpha course we prayed for a lady who returned home and received a phone call from her daughter later that same day. On the phone it was not long before her daughter asked her mum, 'What has happened to you? Your voice has changed.' Being filled with the Holy Spirit may not be immediately apparent to us, but to others it is often all too evident.

The reason for giving you our personal testimony is because churches are shaped by leaders, and leaders tend to lead out of their experience. Or, to put it another way, as leaders we want to lead others into what we have discovered to be true in our experience. Indeed, it is difficult to lead people beyond our own experience. We know that Father God wants everyone to have an awareness of His love for them, and that it is the Spirit of adoption (Romans 8:14-15, 23) that gives us that assurance and the experience of His love being 'poured ... into our hearts' (Romans 5:5). It is that knowledge and experience that has shaped how I lead.

One of our home group leaders, Kerri, first experienced being filled with the Spirit at a church on an RAF base before she moved to Norfolk. As others were prayed for she felt what she described as 'a wave of power'. Kerri had lots of questions but says, 'I knew I was special, that I was loved. Loved unconditionally. I knew then that God was real.' We know that Father God wants to equip us with all that we need to be effective as His disciples. We know that He is committed to forging our character to resemble His as the fruit of the Spirit is developed in us (Galatians 5:22-23). We know that everyone is able to participate in the gifts and ministries given by the Spirit (1 Corinthians 12:7). So, we intentionally press into all of this through our teaching.

But teaching has to be applied to be effective. If we believe, as we do, that more of the Spirit is something that we are invited into, then we have to make space for 'asking' and 'receiving' (Luke 11:13). We usually start our gatherings with an invitation to the Spirit to come;[137] we may during our worship intentionally press in to making space for 'more', and we will always end our gatherings by inviting the Spirit to confirm the word that has been spoken or preached. All of this gives the opportunity for the Spirit to do something outside any constraint that we might put around Him, and gives freedom for Him to speak or act.

I can remember the very first time I invited the Spirit to come in a public gathering. It felt scary. The Spirit comes when others invite Him to – but would He come when I asked? The answer, of course, was and is – yes! But we have to overcome our fear and be prepared to lose control.

What does being discipled by the Spirit look like, and how have we created a culture that enables this to happen? It is as

[137] God is always present with us (Psalm 139:7) but saying, 'Come Holy Spirit,' acknowledges our need of God at that particular time and is an invitation to Him to come and fill us afresh with His Spirit (Luke 11:13; Ephesians 5:18). There is always more of the Spirit available to us (John 3:34).

simple as making space for the Spirit to move. I remember Paul Harcourt, UK leader of New Wine, making the point that 'of course God is at work in every service, but are people leaving them empowered for mission? How much freedom do we give God to move in ways that we might not have predicted? Do we ask Him to come and, if we do, do we wait to see what He wants to do?'[138] We can find space to apply this in all sorts of traditions and ways of being church.

We have to give opportunity for teaching to be put into practice and experienced. Jesus discipled the Twelve by sending them out to do things that were beyond their natural ability: 'Heal those there who are ill and tell them, "The kingdom of God has come near to you"' (Luke 10:9), and He 'gave them power and authority to drive out all demons' (Luke 9:1). They had to trust God for protection (10:3) and provision (v4), and were instructed to find people of peace (v6) – those who would listen and welcome them.

Jesus Himself often attracted attention by doing something that demanded explanation. Nicodemus came to Him on that basis: 'no one could perform the signs you are doing if God were not with him' (John 3:2). So, when we meet together we make space for the gifts of the Spirit to be exercised.

When we gather in any context, there is always the opportunity for people to receive personal prayer in the power of the Holy Spirit for healing, guidance in decisions to be taken, or wisdom for any other circumstance of life in which they find themselves. Often this is accompanied with laying-on of hands.[139] There are usually testimonies to encountering the presence of God, perhaps a word of encouragement, healing received, a sense of peace or an assurance of being loved. All of this gives us confidence to expect God to speak to us in our

---

[138] This was in a New Wine circular letter.
[139] Laying-on of hands is a biblical model used often by Jesus (eg Luke 4:40) and the early Church to impart healing (Acts 28:8), anoint for leadership (Acts 6:6) or infill with the Holy Spirit (Acts 8:15-18).

homes, communities and workplaces, and provides models of how to pray for people outside a church setting.

We encourage testimonies and use these to encourage people to receive prayer. One Sunday we heard the story of a man who ran his own vehicle repair garage and who had damaged his shoulder while working. His wife had prayed for him and it had been instantly healed. He gave this story and then we invited people with shoulder problems to receive prayer. During this time somebody had a word that there was someone present with a painful right wrist. Another person who had a painful left wrist then asked for prayer. Guess whose wrist was healed! We don't exactly know how God is going to work, but creating a culture of faith and making space for Him to do so is essential.

There are six specific areas in which we have particularly experienced the enabling of the Holy Spirit – we shall explore the first of these now and cover the other five in the next chapter.

The Spirit disciples us into healing the sick

The Greek root words (*soteria, sozo*), translated in the Bible as 'salvation', are rich in meaning and can be variously translated as healing, wholeness and deliverance. It is in the nature of God to heal (Exodus 15:26). When a person turns to Christ, receives His forgiveness and is filled with the Spirit, physical healing can sometimes be the outcome.

Healing has always been part of the Fountain's formation and story. Derek was given two weeks to live. He was diagnosed with prostate cancer and had a malignant tumour clearly visible in his abdomen. His wife, Sonia, had been praying for more than thirty years for him to become a Christian but he was proving a hard nut to crack – even then not wanting anyone from 'church' to visit him. But this proved to be the *kairos*[140] moment for the shell to be opened up, and Sonia had the great joy of leading her husband in a prayer welcoming Jesus into his life and trusting Him for the future. As a consequence we were now allowed not only to visit him, but also pray for him. The whole church prayed. Our prayers were answered. The tumour miraculously (according to his medical consultant) turned into an abscess and Derek regained his strength and weight. He was discharged in time to come to our Christmas carol service. He was advised that he would never walk again but once again God did more than he could have expected and he regained his mobility. But it was what God did in him that was just as remarkable. I spoke recently to Alison, his daughter, who told me that he was 'a totally transformed person with a real joy that was evident to all'. While he was in hospital we prayed for Sonia, who at the time had a painful back. Her pain went and, ironically, Derek was more impressed with her healing than his own. He said afterwards that he would never have believed it had he not seen it! 'Blessed are those who have not seen and yet have believed' (John 20:29).

The Holy Spirit is committed to discipling us into the miraculous, and it is the more evidently supernatural gifts, such as healing and the prophetic, that mark a church out as being 'charismatic', and so perhaps unsurprisingly these feature in our experience and growth. Moses was called by God to raise his staff and stretch out his hand over the waters (Exodus 14:16). It was a relatively simple thing for him to do. Parting the waves was the somewhat more difficult part. But that was God's job. Laying hands on a person and praying for them to be healed is our job. Healing them is God's.

Derek's story is an illustration. Testimonies and stories of God's power to heal have punctuated our own story. I shall

---

[140] *Kairos* is a 'now' moment in time that requires us to make an immediate response (eg Mark 1:14-15). I shall say more about this in Chapter 11.

always remember having a conversation with an elderly lady at church in the mid-1980s. I asked her how she was, and in her reply she said something like, 'Well, it's all rather embarrassing, but I am struggling with incontinence. I can't rely upon myself any more and I no longer feel able to go out for any length of time.' I was struck by her vulnerability and willingness to open up to a young (this is thirty-five years ago!) man. We prayed together and the following week she was back in church. I was somewhat tentatively going to ask her how her week had been when she approached me with a big smile to say that she had been free of problems all week. Praise the Lord! I was reminded of the woman who approached Jesus from behind, touched the hem of His cloak and was healed (Mark 5:27). This lady too had overcome her sense of shame and the Lord had seen her distress and heard her cry.

I remember Pippa and I being invited a few years ago to lead a weekend mission at a church in Northern Ireland. A lady was there who had suffered severe back pain for much of her married life owing to arthritis in her spine. Her husband was not with her as he was not yet a Christian and didn't 'do' church. We prayed for her that God would come and straighten her spine and heal her pain. She cited some measure of improvement and went home. So often we have absolutely no idea about the outcome of our prayers, but on this occasion she was back again in the evening – this time with her husband. She had not been totally healed but the improvement had been so great that her husband came to meet the people who had prayed and to visit the place where it had happened, which was his local church.

We do not know the end of that particular story. All we can do is be obedient in the opportunities that come our way, sow the seed of the kingdom and leave it to the Holy Spirit to water and bring about the growth (1 Corinthians 3:6).

One day Simon and Becca came to see us. They were a young married couple who had been worshipping with us for a few years, were excellent leaders of one of our home groups and sensed that it was time for them to start a family. However, they were having some difficulties in conceiving and had sought medical counsel, which had identified that Becca suffered from polycystic ovaries. This reminded us of another couple for whom we had prayed. For similar reasons the couple had been unable to conceive naturally. On that occasion, we had prayed for them on our sofa and exactly nine months later they gave birth to a little girl – although conception did not take place on our sofa! This was our testimony and we shared it with Simon and Becca to raise faith and expectation, and invited God to come and do it again.

Reflecting on this time, Simon recalled, 'As we prayed, God gave us a word that we would experience a revelation in our lives.' Somewhat unusually, God gave me a picture of a calendar with an arrow pointing to a date, 21st April, which I somewhat tentatively shared with them.[141] They pick up the story:

Eventually the 21st came and went without anything obviously special happening. We made it to our fertility appointment and were told categorically that we would not conceive naturally, having tried for many years before. They did a baseline blood test before starting treatment to assist us in falling pregnant and it was positive, suggesting Becca was pregnant. They were not convinced and sent us for a repeat test a few days later and explained that if the level had increased, then we were pregnant. Indeed a few days later the numbers were soaring. This alone was amazing and we were so grateful to God for the miracle He had performed but the relevance of 21st April was still unclear. We went for an ultrasound to confirm the pregnancy and during the scan the technician took some measurements and from that

---

[141] We usually have a policy of 'no dates, fates or mates' as a discipline upon any prophetic words or insights shared. Hence my hesitation.

estimated the day of conception. When she told us April 21st we nearly fell off our chairs.

God is so good!

Engaging in the healing ministry is for everyone – not just church leaders or the spiritually elite, a type of SAS task force called upon in emergency. Our job is to train and equip all to heal the sick. Jesus healed the sick. There was no disease or sickness too difficult for Him to deal with. We might say, 'Well, that's all very well, but that's Jesus – He is God.' We would probably all agree that Jesus is in a league by Himself. He is God (John 1:1, 18). But it is so vital for us to grasp that His three years of ministry on earth, living in our midst, were spent as a human being filled with the power of the Holy Spirit initially poured out at the time of His baptism in the river Jordan (Luke 3:22; Philippians 2:7-8). Therefore, we can look to Jesus as the model for how to live a fully human life empowered by His Spirit in every way, and the more we look to Him and understand our position in Him, the more activity of the kingdom we shall see around us.

We begin to see this working out in the first disciples who were released into praying for the sick and proclaiming the good news of the kingdom (Luke 9:1-6). We see it in the response to the sending-out of the seventy-two in Luke 10. Having been sent out to proclaim the kingdom and heal the sick, they return to Jesus full of wonder and awe that 'even the demons submit to us in your name' (Luke 10:17).

This reminds us of two things. First, there is no power in our name to heal the sick. The healing ministry is always first and foremost the ministry of Jesus through us. Second, it is our eternal destiny that is the priority. At the time Jesus gave a salutary reminder to His fledgling followers: 'Do not rejoice that the spirits submit to you, but rejoice that your names are written in heaven' (Luke 10:20).

After His resurrection and the forty days He then spent with His disciples, Jesus prepared to return to His Father and gathered His followers for one last coaching session. It proved to be brief. First, He invited them to operate out of His *exousia* (authority) rather than their own (Matthew 28:18-20). John uses this same Greek word in his Gospel, which is translated as 'right' when He proclaims that 'to those who believed in his name [Jesus], he gave the [*exousia*] to become children of God' (John 1:12). Healing the sick is part of our inheritance as the children of God. When we place ourselves under His Lordship we come under His authority and have His co-permission to heal the sick. Our confidence in engaging in the healing ministry of Jesus increases when we recognise the authority that we carry in His name.

Then, as part of His final briefing, Jesus pointed to something else too. He said to the assembled people, 'stay in the city until you have been clothed with power from on high' (Luke 24:49). So they waited for ten days until the Day of Pentecost came and they were all filled with the power that had been promised 'from on high'. After the Spirit was poured out at Pentecost, the book of Acts testifies that the whole world was turned upside down as 'unschooled, ordinary' people (Acts 4:13) saw the power of God fall upon their communities through their own hands.

So our job is to equip and release everyone into the ministry that is rightfully theirs to inherit. We train a prayer ministry team who are the 'go to' people when we gather as church. But the supernatural is not to be locked up within either the church or the prayer ministry team. The challenge is for us all to pray for the sick to be healed in our homes, workplaces or streets. Just this last Sunday (as I write) we heard of the story of Rysia, whose car broke down. The breakdown recovery service was duly called and Rysia and her sister Mysia were transported home, with their car on the back of the recovery vehicle. The driver mentioned that some members of his family were seriously ill. So, with his permission, Rysia prayed for them there and then. It has become a natural part of everyday life for members of the

185

church family to pray for those they encounter who are suffering from sickness and ill-health.

Our experience suggests that when people first step out in obedience to pray for the sick, God seems to hear and respond to those initial tentative steps, just as a good parent will reach out in encouragement to the toddler learning to walk. Not always – I remember John Wimber saying that he prayed for people for six months before he saw anything at all[142] – but often. I recall a GP, who had recently come to faith and was doing Alpha, praying for someone's knee to be healed and being amazed that God seemed to make it better as a result of his simple prayer. God loves simplicity and faith.

Sooner or later, though, we will encounter the disappointment of our prayers not being answered in the way we had hoped. As a young Christian I remember the Church across the world praying for David Watson[143] to be healed of cancer and the shock when he wasn't. We do worship a God of the miraculous but also a God of the mystery. There are times when we simply do not know why our prayers seem to go unanswered; then we are called to put our trust in a God who is still good and sets time within an eternal perspective.

The 'now and not yet' of the kingdom is enough of a perspective for me. The kingdom is near, it is at hand, it is within me, it is a daily reality, and the more we pray for in the here and now, the more we shall see. But, as the writer of Ecclesiastes says, there is a season to everything – 'a time to be born and a time to die' (Ecclesiastes 3:2). Even Lazarus eventually had to die. We pray and sometimes people get better at once. Sometimes gradually and sometimes not at all. Our ultimate healer is God and He is our ultimate destination. One day '"There will be no more death" or mourning or crying or pain,

---

[142] This was at the teaching sessions on the Holy Spirit referred to in Chapter 9.

[143] David Watson was an Anglican priest, evangelist and author who died in 1984. Approaching his death he wrote *Fear No Evil* (London: Hodder & Stoughton, 1994).

for the old order of things [will have] passed away' (Revelation 21:4). In the meantime we must live with the mystery as well as the miraculous.

One Sunday morning a few months after I had succeeded Martin, Joan walked through our doors. Her husband, Brian, had recently completed an Alpha course with us and she was interested in exploring the church. She invited her friend Lorraine to come along with her the following week. Over time, Brian and Joan, Lorraine and her husband, Steve, all joined the church and we got to know and appreciate each one of them. Joan in particular was such a wonderful source of encouragement with a vibrant faith – a spiritual 'mother' to Lorraine especially.

Then one day I received a call to say that Joan had been diagnosed with terminal cancer and had been given just a few months to live. We mobilised as much prayer as we could muster. We visited her and prayed our best possible prayers. We all hoped and even fasted. But all to no avail. Within a few weeks Joan had to be relinquished into the loving arms of her Father by all those who knew and loved her – including ourselves. It seemed inopportune. It has to be said that Joan herself was the most accepting of all. She seemed to realise that this was her time and she was ready and at peace to move on to the next stage of her journey. It would take us a while to recover, but it didn't deter us from praying for the next person who came our way in need of healing.

During our trip to India with the interns I referred to earlier, we met Rachel. Rachel had recently become a Christian from a Hindu background, and was now living in community with her new church family. We got to know Rachel well. She was very outgoing and made friends with the team easily. We all quickly grew to love her as one of our own. Then one day we were told that she had been taken ill in the night and was in hospital. We visited her and prayed for her. She was diagnosed as having had a severe epileptic fit and the hospital could not do anything further for her. She was discharged into the care of her church family and, despite our best prayers, we were woken in the middle of the night with the news that she had died. The pastor was concerned that as we had been involved in praying for her, members of her family might seek us out for reprisals.

As we were in any event due to leave the following day we were encouraged to leave immediately before news broke. This seemed to be the wisdom of God, so we roused everyone and set off for our next destination – about a six-hour drive to the north. Dawn broke a few hours into our journey, and we paused to admire it and also to give ourselves some space to process all that had happened. As I gazed upon this wonderful dawn unfolding before my eyes, I remembered the last prayer that I had prayed over Rachel late the previous evening. It was that when she woke up the following morning she would do so to a dawn more radiant than she had ever experienced, a brand-new day and a healthy body and mind. I hadn't quite imagined my prayers to be answered in this way, but surely this is our ultimate hope: that death has been 'swallowed up in victory … through our Lord Jesus Christ' (1 Corinthians 15:54, 57, KJV). Who can imagine what the Lord has prepared for us when we finally meet Him face to face?

Some reflections here are relevant and helpful from James Casson, a young family doctor, diagnosed with a terminal illness, who told his story in *Dying: The Greatest Adventure of My Life*. He comments:

> What are my feelings as I write these final paragraphs? Firstly, surprise that I have survived long enough to finish it. Some days I have felt so ill that it seemed I could not possibly awake the next morning. Secondly, a conviction that even if one person benefits through it the effort will have been worthwhile. Thirdly, the unceasing awareness of the spiritual world as my body weakens, of music on the distant hill becoming louder, of the vision of glory

becoming more clear now that my journey is almost over.[144]

He concludes:

> The conflict of whether 'I was doing everything correctly' did trouble me. Release came with the realisation that the whole issue was out of my hands. One morning I had a clear picture that I was in a boat. Before, when asking for healing, it was as though I was in a punt where one stands at one end pushing on the punt pole and steering with more or less expertise. Afterwards, I was in a rowing boat, my back to the direction I was going, but travelling in a much more leisurely fashion. The great joy was that the Lord was at the tiller, his face gently smiling and his eyes twinkling as he quietly guided me to my destination. Was I healed? Yes, I believe I was.[145]

The healing and deliverance ministry entrusted to us by Jesus is a learning process for us all, and we can trust the Holy Spirit to disciple us into it.

---

[144] James H Casson, *Dying: The Greatest Adventure of My Life* (London: Christian Medical Fellowship, 1980), p34.
[145] Ibid, p37.

10
Walking by the Spirit

*For the Spirit God gave us does not make us timid, but
gives us power, love and self-discipline.*
(2 Timothy 1:7)

The New Testament presents a dynamic picture of life in the
Spirit. We are called to 'live by the Spirit' and to 'keep in step
with the Spirit' (Galatians 5:25); to 'have [our] minds set on what
the Spirit desires' (Romans 8:5). Simeon was 'moved by the
Spirit' to be in the right place at the right time (Luke 2:27). Just
as Jesus was 'led by the Spirit' (Matthew 4:1), so there is an
expectation that the children of God will be 'led by the Spirit'
(Romans 8:14). There is an overwhelming sense presented
throughout the New Testament that the Spirit of God, 'who
raised Jesus from the dead' and who now lives in us (Romans
8:11), will not only radically transform us into the likeness of
God but will also endow us with all that we need to do His work.
This, of course, relates to the whole of our life but, in this
chapter, we shall focus on the five further specific areas in which
we have particularly experienced the discipling work of the Holy
Spirit.

The Spirit disciples us into prophetic ministry

Like the ministry of healing, the prophetic is a ministry for all of us, not just a few (1 Corinthians 14:1). The Spirit enables us to hear what God is saying to us. We can know the thoughts of God about ourselves, other people, circumstances and events, the Church and the nation or even the world. As with the healing ministry, there will be those for whom there is a specific anointing and calling to exercise the office of a prophet. But we can all expect the Lord to speak to us and through us to others.

Some eight years ago, early one morning, as I wrestled with feelings of being unable to carry all of the responsibilities upon me at the time, I distinctly sensed God the Father speaking to me – not in an audible voice, but in a way that indelibly printed the words in my mind and upon my heart. The words were quite simply, 'You are loved. You are precious. You are Mine.' Words like this are intended to strengthen our resolve and deepen our sense of working from our identity and position as sons and daughters, deeply cherished and loved for who we are.

Four years ago, I was hosting a mini-conference for a group of Swiss pastors. One of them asked if he could pray for me – an offer I rarely turn down! He didn't ask me, 'What would you like me to pray for?' – he just went ahead and prayed. As he did, he sensed the Lord wanting me to know that I was like a tree, that I should stay where I was, and not 'become a grandfather somewhere else'. Since then the word 'grandfather' has been a significant one. Not only in the sense of being a grandfather in the natural to two energetic grandsons, but also reinforcing a calling to this particular place and people – not necessarily forever but at least for now.

As I write, I remember praying, several years ago, for a lady weighed down by a deep sense of shame after a failed marriage. As I prayed for her, I had a strong sense of her as a bride and Jesus as her bridegroom – it was a clear picture in my mind. I passed this impression on to her and we prayed for a little while longer. I know this picture brought her tremendous healing over the years and transformed her understanding of who she was in

Christ. The 'now' word of God when handled well brings healing, life and purpose.

At a more global and strategic level, I can think of several significant prophecies over the past fifty or so years that have been spoken over the United Kingdom. One that particularly comes to mind is the prophecy given by Jean Darnall[146] in 1967 on her first visit to the UK (at this time she was pastoring a church in the US with her husband, Elmer). According to the paraphrase of a transcript that I have, in her vision:

> The British Isles were covered in mist (a green haze), and Jean Darnall saw lots of pinpricks of light piercing through. As she looked, they turned out to be fires breaking out all over the nation, from Scotland in the north to Land's End in the south. As these God-lit fires were joined together they burned brighter. As she continued to pray, she saw lightning and explosions of fire and then rivers of fire flowing from north to south; from Scotland, Ireland and Wales into England and some of the streams of fires crossed the Channel into Europe, while others stopped. She had the distinct impression that there would be two moves of God. The first would be the renewal of Christian faith and fullness of the Holy Spirit within the Church … This renewal of life in the Church would spread outside resulting in a public awakening … This move of God would be a national spiritual awakening, which would move into every level of the nation's life.[147]

In May 2009 Jean spoke at the New Wine leaders' conference, reminding us all of this prophecy and also encouraging us to be a 'sent people', declaring, 'The harvest is ready. It is not tomorrow, it is not next year – it is now, My children, that the

---

146 American pastor who exercised an international prophetic ministry. She died in 2019, aged ninety-six.
147 Sourced from Call to Prayer, call2prayer.co.uk (accessed 14th April 2021).

harvest is here.' Such prophecies have a complete fulfilment yet to come but, while we wait, they give hope, remind us of promise and encourage us to press on, always looking for the green shoots of revival.

The exercise of the gift of prophecy is seen by Paul as being for the purpose of 'strengthening, encouraging and comfort' (1 Corinthians 14:3). So, this is the primary test we apply in weighing what people 'hear' and 'see'. There are other tests, the simplest of which is perhaps, 'Does this sound like the sort of thing that Jesus would say? Does it resemble His character, glorify Him, release healing and wholeness? Does it seem good to us?'

It's not for us to understand the significance or meaning of what we receive for others. I remember leading a group of ten-year-olds in a time of waiting on God. We had encouraged them that one of the ways God can speak to us is by giving us a picture. One child said that they had a picture of a toilet, which, as you can imagine, caused a good deal of hilarity among the group and could easily have been dismissed as a 'childish' response. But instead it proved to be childlike and was of significance for one of the helpers in the group.

On Sundays, when we have been able to gather together, we value creating space for God to move and speak. Before the morning service begins, a team meets to pray and invite the Spirit to lay on our hearts anything the Father wants to do in our midst. Later, these 'words' are shared with the congregation and regularly, Sunday by Sunday, there is a response to them. There are times during our worship together when individuals in the congregation will sense God prompting them to share a thought, word or picture.[148] We have at times paused during our worship to hear what God wants to say to us and invited those present to share anything they feel God is saying to them that is

---

[148] This has been our model until Covid-19. However, the principle of listening to God and being responsive to His voice has continued to be reflected in our livestreaming of services on our YouTube channel and making use of the 'Chat' facility.

for us all. Sometimes what is given publicly is sifted through the leader, but other times an open microphone is made available. All that is said is always assessed by the criteria of 1 Corinthians 14:3 – does it strengthen, encourage or bring comfort? Not everything given is particularly revelatory, but it gives space for trial and error and enables us to hear the 'now' word which otherwise would be hidden.

Creating space to wait upon God for His agenda during our times of meeting together is an area that I feel we have never done well enough. Annually, at the beginning of the year, we would set aside a morning service to do this, but I'm sure there have been many times when the Spirit has been saying, 'Hang on. Just linger here for what I want to say or do.' As leader, I have always been mindful of what needs to be said and done, especially during our main Sunday services, and that can constrain our ability to make space for silence and inactivity – putting into practice, 'Be still, and know that I am God' (Psalm 46:10).

A few years ago, Carol started to lead her home group in times of worship and resting in the presence of God. The home group under the leadership of Martin and Wendy sensed the Lord wanting to make this model and experience available to others. So once a month they moved their home group into the worship centre and opened it up to all on a Monday evening. It grew, and our worship team took on responsibility for its leadership and it was integrated into our evening programme of Sunday services. Appropriately called Closer, it provides a more relaxed setting than is possible on a Sunday morning, with coffee, cake and bean bags available so that people can just rest and soak in the presence of God, read Scripture, or give and receive personal prayer. It is a much-valued opportunity to press the pause button and draw closer in intimacy to our Father God. A team leads us in sung worship with space for people to engage in painting or other creative activities, make prophetic contributions, share Scripture, pray or simply spend time resting in the presence of God. When we gather together, there is an open microphone so that people can come forward and speak out what God is saying. Closer is another way of making space to facilitate the discipling work of the Spirit in us all.[149]

The Spirit is committed to discipling us in our relationship with God

The Spirit seeks to glorify the Father and the Son and draw us into the intimacy of the heart of the Trinitarian circle. The icon of the Trinity painted in the fifteenth century by the Russian artist Andrei Rublev captures this invitation.[150] It depicts the three angels who visited Abraham at the Oak of Mamre and is widely interpreted as a symbol of the Trinity. The Father, Son and Spirit are shown reclining around a table, each deferring to the other and implicitly inviting us to enter into the picture for ourselves by joining them in the space made available at the table.

Times of worship enable us to respond to this invitation and find our place at the table. Of course, worship is far more than just singing hymns or songs. We are called to love Him for Himself alone, not for what He can give or do for us. William Temple defined worship as

> the submission of all our nature to God. It is the quickening of conscience by his holiness; the nourishment of mind with his truth; the purifying of imagination by his beauty; the opening of the heart to his love; the surrender of will to his purpose – all this gathered up in adoration.[151]

Such a wonderful way of expressing the breadth and depth of what it means to be a worshipper. In my experience, though,

---

[149] Closer moved online during Covid-19, with the worship team facilitating a monthly Sunday evening opportunity to spend time in God's presence.

[150] Type in 'Andrei Rublev Trinity' on Google to see this icon.

[151] www.goodreads.com/quotes/1543945 (accessed 29th January 2021).

our times of sung worship have been an essential part in helping us express this adoration and love for God and engage with Him. As the psalmist puts it, we 'enter his gates with thanksgiving and his courts with praise' (Psalm 100:4). It is in these times that we often create the time and space we need to encounter His presence, receive His love and have our minds nourished, our imaginations purified, our consciences quickened and our wills surrendered to His.

Encounter begins when we move beyond the words or music and can focus all of our attention on the person to whom we are singing, and worship leaders play a crucial part in facilitating this. We have been richly blessed in this regard with both musical gifting and worship leaders. Currently our team is led by John and Becky and Carol. All three were prompted by the Spirit to learn how to play an instrument for the purpose of leading worship. All three have been part of our journey since the early part of Martin Down's incumbency in the formative years that led to the emergence of the Fountain of Life.

As a sixteen-year-old, Becky found herself playing the organ at the parish church. A couple of years later, she stepped out as one of a few who could lead us in worship, playing the guitar and helping us take our first faltering steps in having a more informal time of sung worship, stringing some songs together. She taught herself guitar by having a copy of *Mission Praise* with chords above the lyrics. Becky then went to university, and during her degree she did an internship with New Wine at St Andrew's Chorleywood.

John was Becky's fiancé, and as he was filled with the Spirit during one of his visits, he experienced a deep sense of the love and acceptance of the Father. He went home and opened the Bible at a random page, where God spoke to him powerfully through the words the Father spoke to Jesus: 'You are my Son, whom I love; with you I am well pleased' (Mark 1:11). He received a new hunger to worship and he learned to play the guitar. This seemed to be a supernatural gifting, as he hadn't done anything musical up until that point – not even singing – but was accelerated in his ability beyond a natural timeframe.

Carol, too, has been involved since the beginning. She moved into the village and could play the guitar. She offered to play in church and attended a group to find out more about becoming a Christian. She came to Christ and was filled with the Spirit. She joined the worship team.

During the 1990s we held a monthly worship and teaching event called First Saturday. This was key in deepening our experience of life in the Spirit and developing the confidence of the worship team in leading times of continuous worship. It released a space for hearing from God and encountering His presence. It was a place of development and growth for the worship team and the release of many others into leadership. It all lay foundations for what was to come.

The team John, Becky and Carol lead, almost thirty years later, includes professional musicians, others trained to Grade Eight in their chosen instrument and still others who are self-taught or just stepping out. All of them are worshippers first, worship leaders second and 'professional' musicians third. They lead out of the integrity of their relationship with God. They are our 'lead' worshippers. There is a real authenticity about their life as a worshipping community.

John and Becky and Carol have invested themselves in creating a family within a family. The worship team, which includes visuals and PA, dance and banners, now numbers forty plus.[152] They have prioritised the value of community. As much as they can, they 'do life together'. They encourage, teach and pastor the team. As they spend time eating together, praying together, socialising together and building real community with each other, it builds family and sets the atmosphere for our gatherings. They prefer one another (Romans 12:10, KJV),

---

[152] During Covid-19, the team organised themselves into four bands (socially distanced) to take responsibility for one Sunday per month. The technical team proved to be a huge strength in enabling us to livestream services and provide high-quality recordings.

making space for each other to lead and grow, following a model of appointing joint worship leaders at services and events.

One of the benefits of strength of team is the ability to rotate leadership – no one person needs to be in the band every week. They can take time out and receive as part of the congregation. When the church gathers, we become an extension of this wonderful worshipping community as we all seek to worship 'in the Spirit and in truth' (John 4:24).

Worshipping 'in the Spirit and in truth' involves our bodies as well as our minds and souls. Often as the Spirit moves upon us as a congregation we find people raising their hands to various levels, kneeling, resting or dancing. I always feel happier when there is a diversity of response to the coming of the Spirit. For me, it affirms the authenticity of the movement of God. He is so creative and we are so unique in our emotional, spiritual and physical wiring that it makes more sense for there to be a very individual and unique response to the activity of the Spirit.

It's natural for there to be a physical response to receiving the love God has for us. We are mere mortals – God is pretty awesome! On one Alpha course when we invited the Holy Spirit to come I was aware of one lady standing, eyes closed, hands stretched out to receive from God. She was saying over and over again, 'These wonderful arms of love.' Eventually she folded her arms around herself and this time simply said, 'These wonderful arms of love. They are for me.' A profound experience of being loved by the God who made the stars.[153] We don't have that profound experience every time we worship, but if we are singing songs to glorify God, it is not such a strange reaction to want to lift our hands up as a physical expression. Or if we are singing about receiving the love of God, it seems perfectly appropriate for us to hold our hands out in a receiving manner as a physical sign that we believe what we are singing and are engaging in our response.

[153] Genesis 1:16.

We have banners available for people to use during our worship and space for dance. Sometimes we invite artists to paint during worship. Some of these paintings have been kept as permanent reminders of God's call upon us as a church. Others relate to specific seasons in our life together and still others are simply for that moment or for someone to take away with them. The Spirit works in a diverse and creative way.

In our worship together, we are mindful of Paul's instructions in 1 Corinthians 14:39-40 to 'be eager to prophesy, and do not forbid speaking in tongues. But everything should be done in a fitting and orderly way.' Making space for Him and stewarding the activity of the Spirit is our job. Turning up and releasing the gifts is His. Where there is freedom in worship for God to move, there is always a sense of excitement that something unexpected might happen. Someone might be healed, a word of encouragement or reassurance might be given, a profound sense of God's presence might be experienced.

Sometimes in the midst of our worship we have found ourselves overflowing into words that the Spirit enables us to speak. Paul refers to it in 1 Corinthians 14 as speaking 'in tongues'. It's a language given to us by God that is intended to enrich our relationship with Him. It is a language of prayer and worship, and it enables us to be extended beyond the limits of our own native language. Mostly it is given for our private use, but when someone speaks out in this way in public, then we usually pause our worship and wait for an interpretation – again in line with Paul's teaching in 1 Corinthians 14. While not everyone will speak in tongues, nor is it an essential sign of being baptised in the Spirit, it is a gift the Father loves to give and is often one of the first gifts people receive. At the same time we know many who have repeatedly asked for the gift, are open to receiving it but for unknown reasons have not yet received it.

God loves to reward perseverance. Just this week I was talking to a lady who had asked for the gift of tongues repeatedly for many years. Just before Christmas, she found herself in a Catholic church in a small mountain village in France. It was a place that seemed to her like an 'open heaven', a place where she sensed the presence of God so strongly, and as she stood in front of a rather ornate and large nativity scene, she found herself speaking in tongues as she prayed for renewal and revival in France. It reminded both of us of a prophetic picture once given by the French worship team Flamme at New Wine many years ago of an eagle soaring and areas of light being punched into the darkness over Europe, including France.

It has been wonderful to see the way in which some of our young people have developed in leading worship within our church. There has been a succession of worship leaders emerging from our young people over the years. John and Becky led a youth home group out of which a number of young people emerged into the worship team. Alex was one of these, and he looks back at this time fondly:

> I was introduced to the Holy Spirit. He tutored me in how to usher in His presence using music and sung worship. I learned from all the musicians and leaders but we learned together as we 'workshopped' through those times. I treasure that period and thank God that I was so blessed to be a part of His movement in Ashill. I experienced what it was to see into and shift the spiritual architecture in a place. Incredible how His design features many different elements and journeys and I'm sure He was doing so much in so many different ways and in many different people! But that is what He was doing in me. Yes, it was a chance to learn how to be a skilled Levite[154] but it was more about learning how I minister to Him. How I minister to and partner with the Holy Spirit. I think this is why my heart for worship teams and people called to minister is so strong! I feel blessed that I

---

[154] Under the Mosaic covenant, the Levites were set aside to minister before God at first in the tabernacle, and then in the temple, enabling worship through the system of sacrifices and offerings (see, for example, Numbers 18:23; 2 Chronicles 5:4-6; Ezra 6:20).

was a part of that time and am energised for the future because of it.

There is a culture within the worship team of always looking for the next person to emerge, investing in them and releasing them into their gift and ministry. Our first youth worker, Martin, built on John and Becky's work by starting a youth band called Jam, which gathered young people around music and worship but shifted the focus to engage in mission and outreach. This band, led by the young people, took worship songs out into the community. They led worship at open-air services and sang at local street carnivals, fetes and other secular venues. They broke new ground by entering a secular 'open bands night' at a nearby music school, singing Christian songs.

A few years later, after returning from university, our son, Simon, one of the leaders of this band, joined the worship team and is now one of our worship leaders. He has a great ability to compose music for lyrics written by members of the church. He married Louise, who he met at the very last Living Water event, and she joined the worship team too. Louise came with a beautiful voice and a heart for worship and also had experience of being part of a Christmas musical presentation of the gospel organised in partnership with Tearfund. It required the support of schools in the local area to make space for schoolchildren to learn the songs and participate in the performances. Simon and Louise worked with our Kidz Klub team, schools and other churches across mid-Norfolk to replicate it here and produced *One Christmas* and, two years later, *Waiting for Christmas*, both musical productions of the Christmas story. All of this enriched our ability to take the gospel out into the wider community, increased our influence in schools, added to our connections with families and inspired Simon to compose music for other evangelistic occasions, including Christmas Alive.

Rebecca Wilkinson was inspired as a teenager by attending Worship Central, a national programme training worship leaders. She persevered in learning the guitar with Matt Beckett, and is now thriving as a worship intern at Gas Street Church in Birmingham. Simon taught her sister, Kezia, to play the piano and she began to be involved on the worship team. Later, she was at New Wine playing in the band at Boulder Gang, which gave her exposure to something bigger. With Rebecca she went to an event called David's Tent,[155] for a seventy-two-hour time of continuous worship. Kezia has always had a heart for worship, but this gave her a passion for leading worship. She attended a worship leaders' conference hosted by the Fountain of Life with worship leader Neil Bennetts,[156] and out of this she developed a vision to draw together young adults to engage with God in times of free and prophetic worship. This was subsequently fulfilled in an event called The Gathering.

These are all examples of the way in which attending other, larger events during the year releases vision as well as shapes and inspires growth.

Our worship group has incorporated all ages into its bands Sunday by Sunday. Keeva came to church one Sunday morning with her mum, Suzanne. Becky was leading worship, and as her gaze rested upon Keeva, the Lord gave Becky a picture of Keeva standing on the platform leading worship. Keeva was aged five at the time.

Keeva's backstory is that she was diagnosed in utero with a heart condition (AVSD) and her parents were advised that they should consider aborting the pregnancy. They did not and Keeva was born without many of the anticipated complications. However, she still needed major corrective surgery at the age of two, without which she would not live beyond the age of fifteen. The surgery was successful.

Keeva did not start leading worship at the age of five! But at the age of eleven she started attending youth band practice evenings, led by Matt and Grace Schwarzenberger. They prioritised intimacy in worship and helped the group move away

---

155 www.davidstent.net (accessed 29th January 2021).
156 theworshipfoundation.org/about (accessed 29th January 2021).

from any sense of performance culture and, in Keeva's words, 'kept us all grounded'.

Keeva played the guitar but was petrified of appearing in public. The presence of her mum gave her reassurance but it was still hard for her to overcome her fear. For about six months Matt spent time with Keeva, helping her to develop her singing and guitar skills. On their first day together, Matt asked her, 'Why do you want to do this?' and she replied that she really liked Taylor Swift.[157] She said that Swift 'sings and plays her guitar. I really want to do that but do it with worship songs.'

Subsequently she enrolled for professional guitar lessons with a local firm. Asked why she was learning, her answer was, 'I just want to sing worship songs.' She did not know that one of our worship team, Phil, worked for this firm, and so she was amazed when she went for her first lesson and who should walk through the door but Phil. All of this helped her to know that God was on her case and to overcome her fear.

Today, aged fifteen, Keeva has grown into a confident and gifted worship leader. For Keeva, leading worship is about 'doing it with meaning and leading the congregation in the right direction. I love seeing the whole church responding and engaging in worship themselves.'

Maisie has always had a love for singing and music, so it was very natural for her to join the youth band. When I talked to her recently about this, Maisie reflected that 'initially it was about "me" and I felt that I must do everything perfectly – the focus was on performance'. At Intents and then Soul Survivor she found herself connecting with God in a wonderful way through the music and worship: 'I fell in love with worship and sensed the Holy Spirit calling me to help other people find God through worship in the amazing way I was experiencing.' Her attitude changed – now she was totally doing it for God and others rather than herself.

---

157 Taylor Swift is a popular American singer.

I asked Maisie what she would look for in an emerging worship leader:

> Look for someone who is a worshipper in the congregation first before they start being in the band. In growing them as a worship leader, encourage them to be doing it for God and be willing to make changes during worship – singing a song outside the prepared set if what is going on in the room requires it.

At the age of thirteen she already displays a wisdom in leading worship, but then, spiritual maturity is not measured by physical age.

The Spirit disciples us in our relationship with each other

He puts a love in our hearts for one another. He helps us put up with each other, forgive one another and 'be kind … to one another' (Ephesians 4:32). In their book *Implementation Guide: Natural Church Development*,[158] Christian Schwarz and Christoph Schalk have unpacked some principles that have proved helpful to us in informing the life and development of our church. After researching 1,000 growing churches around the world, they identified eight characteristics or qualities that were significant in their growth.[159] The research also revealed that growth is limited by our weakest characteristic. Therefore, in order to grow we need to pay attention to those weaker aspects of our life together. This was illustrated by having a model (beer) barrel built with the staves cut at different lengths. When water was poured into the barrel it obviously overflowed at the lowest point. The message was simple: if we wanted to grow and

---

[158] Christian A Schwarz, Christoph Schalk, *Implementation Guide: Natural Church Development* (Carol Stream, IL: ChurchSmart Resources, 1998).
[159] These are 'empowering leadership; gift-based ministry; passionate spirituality; effective structure; inspiring worship service; holistic small groups; need-oriented evangelism; loving relationships'.

receive more of God's blessings, then increase and strengthen the weakest stave.

Schwarz invited any church that wanted to identify its strengths and weaknesses to complete a survey and send it to his organisation for analysis. So, shortly after his book was published in 1998, we did just that. It revealed, to our surprise, that our weakest point was building 'loving relationships'. We would have rated it as one of our strongest. But the survey was based not on our perception as leaders, but on the perception of members of the church chosen at random to participate. So we began to pray and seek God for this area of our life together.

It's interesting to note now that one of the most common observations we hear about the church from those who visit is how loving and welcoming a community they find us to be. Based on others' experience of us as a church, this is an area that has grown. I am sure, though, there will be those whose experience has not been so great, those who for whatever reason feel overlooked and unloved. No church community is perfect; there is always more that we can do.

It is the Spirit who breaks down the barriers between us and enables us to grow in intimacy and confidence with one another – to 'greet one another with a holy kiss'.[160] We don't put this into practice too literally, but we do show our affection for each other physically, often by exchanging hugs – being mindful of how well we know the person being hugged (and, sadly, not at all at the present time of writing)! Quite rightly, we live in a safeguarding culture and we need to be mindful of staying safe by keeping close physical contact with others in the public arena and not lingering beyond what is appropriate. But let us not be afraid to exercise appropriate touch with one another – it is a language of love, and for many an embrace means more than words.

---

[160] An instruction given four times in the New Testament: Romans 16:16; 1 Corinthians 16:20; 2 Corinthians 13:12; 1 Thessalonians 5:26.

But, of course, loving one another is intended to be much deeper than simply exchanging hugs. *Agape* is the word consistently used in the Bible to describe the love of God and the love Christians have for one another. It is the Holy Spirit who pours this love into our hearts (Romans 5:5) and enables us to love each other sacrificially and form bonds of friendship, even with those who are not like us or who we find difficult to like. My personal experience of this particular family is one of *agape* love. A love that is deeply compassionate, sacrificial and often goes the extra mile.

The Spirit helps disciple us into a lifestyle of financial giving

I have already referred to the extraordinary gift of giving as a community surrounding our purchase of the worship centre. By 2012, a growing staff team and our internship programme was putting pressure on the supporting facilities of our 'home' at The Well. The problem with buildings can be that you grow out of them too quickly. There were at least six people who all needed office space and only two desks between them. We were out of space, not just for storage for all the equipment and supplies necessary to make our activities happen, but we were not able to fit all the workers in. It didn't seem appropriate to start praying for fewer workers so we prayed for more space.

It was at this point that a member of the church asked to come and see me. They had noticed that the house opposite the worship centre was up for sale and offered to buy it for the church. We accepted their offer! This most generous gift enabled us to have a residential facility, increased office and storage space, as well as an extra meeting room.

It needed some refurbishment work, but amazingly the gift allowed for this and a small sum was left over to pump-prime the ongoing maintenance. It was such a clear answer to prayer and has proved to be an extraordinary blessing.

One of the hallmarks of the Fountain throughout has been the way in which people have embraced a constant and sacrificial lifestyle of giving. It overflows. Only the Spirit can produce the heart of generosity that we have witnessed on so many occasions and that has sustained the life of the church week by week.

When teaching about giving, we have often referenced 2 Corinthians 8 and 9. Financial giving should be one of our first priorities and therefore planned (2 Corinthians 9:5, 7). We don't give out of our excess but intentionally prioritise it in our budget. Just as we taught our son when he was younger, there are three pots: a pot for saving, a pot for giving and a pot for spending. Recently I heard a talk in which this third pot was described as 'living' rather than 'spending', which is an even more helpful term to use. How much should go into the giving pot? Paul suggests that our giving should be proportionate (2 Corinthians 8:12) but that it should also be passionate – from the heart (2 Corinthians 8:8; 9:7). This doesn't answer the question in terms of amount, but it gives guidelines as to how to work it out.

Giving should be joyful, and joy-filled giving is evoked by the Spirit at work in us rather than through a response to a law about it. When pressed about tithing, I would always say to those for whom it is an entirely new idea to work towards one-tenth, working it into their budget and having a plan to reach it. But, of course, the chief danger of a target is that it becomes a limit. Even in the Old Testament there were tithes *and* offerings, so 10 per cent is never intended to be the limit, rather more the starting point! After all, if tithing was an Old Testament measure under the law, how much more should we respond to grace? It is a challenge that comes with a promise of blessing (Malachi 3:6-12).

Most years we have held a specific gift day as an opportunity for people to give towards a particular activity or project. Occasionally we have held a gift day simply to balance the books. Each time I stand amazed as this relatively small and not particularly rich family of God's people sacrificially give to reach, and often exceed, the target, which is usually in the order of £25,000 to £40,000. I am always filled with much joy, gratitude and reassurance that discipleship in this area of our lives is alive and well in the church.

Of course, a lifestyle of giving involves more than just giving to the local church. We are finding more of our young people choosing to use their gap year to serve God either in the UK or overseas and needing to be financed. Time and again we, as their family, step up to help turn their vision into reality.

We regularly invite Christian organisations to come and speak to the church and often, as a result, individuals are stirred by the Spirit to sow financially into their work.

The Spirit loves to disciple us into the character of God as revealed supremely in the person of Jesus Christ

In our exploration of the six areas in which we have experienced the enabling of the Holy Spirit, this is perhaps the most important of all. It is perhaps the best way of testing the genuineness of the work of the Holy Spirit, however bizarre the manifestations of the Spirit moving in power can appear. Are we becoming a more loving, more caring, more compassionate people? As we align ourselves with the explicit characteristics associated with life in the Spirit, such as 'love, joy, peace, forbearance, kindness, goodness, faithfulness, gentleness and self-control' (Galatians 5:22-23), so the Spirit loves to make these a reality in our lives. The good news is that there is always more. We can become more loving, more joy-filled, experience more of His peace and grow in our self-control.

We prayed for a man on an early Alpha who confessed that he struggled with uncontrollable anger. Over the following weeks he experienced transformation in this area and found a new strength in self-control. We have prayed for those crippled by anxiety and fear who have found themselves liberated by the love of God and experiencing His peace. We have seen those bound by guilt and shame set free by receiving the forgiveness and acceptance of the Father. We have prayed with those who have become embittered by the hurt done by others and who, as they have released forgiveness and blessing upon those who have caused their pain, have received emotional and physical healing. 'It is for freedom that Christ has set us free' (Galatians 5:1).

Sometimes we have needed to have difficult discipleship conversations with individuals over issues such as sexual behaviour, unforgiveness, serving for identity rather than from it, or unresolved relational issues. There are guidelines for how the body of Christ exercises discipline within itself (Matthew 18:15-17) and at times leaders will need to step in to resolve issues and apply discipline. Always the purpose of this is to preserve the health of the body (1 Corinthians 5:6), 'make disciples' (Matthew 28:19) and release life (1 John 5:16). As we engage in this work, it is good to know that it is the Holy Spirit's job to convict us of our need to change and lead us into repentance. Often it is enough – and wisdom – to step back and give Him time and space in which to work. We are all works in progress, and the good news is that our destiny is to be 'transformed into his image with ever-increasing glory, which comes from the Lord, who is the Spirit' (2 Corinthians 3:18). He is totally committed to bringing the work He has started in us 'to completion' (Philippians 1:6).

One evening at youth band I noticed a man at the back of the worship centre whom I had not met before. He explained that he was the accompanying teacher for a teenager who was in the band but also at a special school for those with behavioural problems. This teacher took the opportunity to say how much the boy had changed since coming to the Fountain. He was able to exercise more self-control over his responses to others and was kinder and more patient. We were able to talk about how these were characteristics of the Spirit and how knowing God had helped this boy become a little bit more like Him.

In concluding this chapter, I would say that being open to the renewing and discipling power of the Spirit of God is entirely responsible for all the fruit we have experienced over the past twenty-five years. He is always faithful and always good.

I am writing this the day after we met Judith. Judith came to a week-long family holiday event that we were involved with more than twenty years ago. During that event we prayed for her to be filled with the Holy Spirit. At the time we had no idea what happened next. Twenty years on, Judith still remembered us praying for her and the difference it made to her to be filled with the Spirit. She felt as if she had been 'brought back to life and was so aware of His presence'. Since then she has been confident in talking about her faith and praying for others to be filled with the Spirit.

It reminded us again, and we do always need to be reminded, that all we need to do is pray, 'Come Holy Spirit,' stand back and watch Jesus build His Church (Matthew 16:18).

11
Leadership Transition

*I tell you that you are Peter, and on this rock I will
build my church, and the gates of Hades will not
overcome it.*
(Matthew 16:18)

In the Greek of the New Testament there is *chronos* time and
then again there is *kairos* time. *Chronos* is used to speak about the
passing of time in general. It's 6.08pm as I write this and it's
Thursday 6th February 2020. That is *chronos* time. It's time as we
know it defined by humankind. *Kairos* time is defined by God.
It's the 'now' of the kingdom. When Jesus said, 'The time has
come … The kingdom of God has come near' (Mark 1:15), He
was referring to *kairos* time. It's a specific time. An 'intervention
of God' time. It's a strategic time, an opportunity that can be
either missed or embraced.

In the summer of 2017, Pippa and I went away for a twenty-
four-hour retreat as part of our regular, planned routine. At its
conclusion we were very sure that the Spirit was saying, 'Now is
the time to pass on the baton.' It was time for me to stop being
the senior leader of the Fountain of Life. This did not mean that
we should return home and immediately step down, but now
was the time for us to be planning towards it and setting a date.
We needed to handle it carefully and within a clearly defined,
public and agreed timeframe.

I had always been clear that passing on the leadership of the church would not be based on *chronos* time. It would not necessarily happen at my appointed retirement age – whether defined by the Church of England or the State. There would come a time when it was right for the church to transition to new leadership, and we trusted that it would also be the right time for us to be released into new activities and a new season. We seemed to have reached this stage in the journey.

From a personal perspective, Pippa and I were not getting any younger – Pippa is a few years older than me – and I am quite sure that in the church at large we need to have greater confidence in releasing younger leaders to lead growing churches. The role of older, more experienced leaders can then be to support and mentor others, encouraging, empowering and supporting them.

A 'life' phrase for me has been the apostle Paul's words to the Corinthian church: 'you do not have many fathers' (1 Corinthians 4:15). There's a deep need for spiritual fathers and mothers to be raised up within the body of Christ. As John Coles puts it:

> For that to happen some of us will need to step down from our decision-making roles. We need to become more like empowering fathers to our now-adult children, rejoicing more in their success than in striving for success ourselves, giving them platforms while we become effective and fervent pray-ers, recognising the joy of being coaches rather than just the joy of being players.[161]

From a church perspective, there were issues of growth to decide upon. We had grown to more than 300 with as many again connected through missional communities. A couple of years earlier, we had turned down the opportunity to buy additional land adjacent to the worship centre. We had

---

[161] John Coles, chair of trustees, New Wine. Quote from a talk John gave a few years ago which I noted. Edited for the purpose of this book.

concluded that the asking price was prohibitive and that door had closed. In any event, a building project did not seem to be the right option. We were committed to growth through missional communities. There were potentially opportunities to plant elsewhere and the Spirit did seem to be blessing us in this and opening up doors. We had already added congregations in a small way at other times on a Sunday, but what should we do about our existing larger Sunday morning gathering? Should this one multiply itself? Were there other options that we should be exploring? These were all positive questions, but they needed imagining for the next five to ten years. Pippa and I would certainly not be in a position to lead the church over that timescale. It felt as if a new leader should be leading the conversation.

The diocese had just nominated us as a resource church and was looking strategically at how it engaged in church planting. I was also mindful of our early history and sensed that moving to a third-generational leadership would help distance the church from its birth pains and make it easier for the church to fulfil this pivotal role as a resource church within the diocese.

There is always a danger of justifying God's decision in human terms. But it seemed to be His voice and that, of course, is always enough. One of the images I have often used in talks on guidance is a scene from one of the Indiana Jones films[162] when Indiana is told to step out from underneath the lion's head. When he reaches the stone lion there is an abyss and apparently no crossing point. But as he acts on the instructions that he has been given and steps out, seemingly into space, a narrow bridge opens up before him and he makes it across to the other side. Faith is often stepping out despite all the evidence to the contrary or, at the very least, not having all the answers as to how the destination will be reached; sometimes

---

[162] *Indiana Jones and the Last Crusade* (1989). Distributors: Paramount Pictures. Leap of Faith clip, www.youtube.com/watch?v=sBBbq2g7yf8 (accessed 15th February 2021).

not even knowing the destination – just knowing we have to step out has to be enough for us. It's all very well in the movies, though, but this was for real.

However, it did make sense of a journey that we had been on since 2013 of reshaping our leadership structure. So, before we move on, something of this story is helpful to tell. At our trustees' vision day in 2013 I had proposed a new leadership structure. At that time, our membership had reached something of a plateau. We had grown and become a place of influence in the region. Generally we were held in high regard, even pointed to as a model (please don't!) and enjoyed favour and provision. But the landscape had changed. There was a new HTB church plant at St Thomas' in Norwich, the permission-giving culture of Fresh Expressions had been embraced by the diocese, our bishops were desperate to see the Church grow and a solution found to the financial crisis. There were other vicars being appointed locally who shared New Wine values. We were no longer a lone voice; there was a cacophony of sound echoing heaven's voice.

We had intentionally released some people to St Stephen's Norwich and others had been called to other churches. We had a growing network influence through both New Wine and the Fountain Network. In partnership with New Wine, we led a New Wine children's workers' network, a worship leaders' network and an internship which now operated in partnership with the New Wine Discipleship Year. Through the Fountain Network we connected to other churches and individuals. I had also received prophetic encouragement at a Fountain Network retreat to commit to networking more fully.

At the time, I felt that both the Fountain of Life Church and the Network needed more leadership time. Networking is relational, hard to quantify or pin down but essential in releasing people into vision, purpose and destiny. At the same time, we could not afford to forget the Fountain's original call and vision to be a Spirit-filled congregation committed to seeing the kingdom come in a way that transforms lives and communities.

We needed a structure that would enable me to respond to the networking opportunities while also making sure the mission and pastoring of the church was not lost. We needed to keep our pioneering edge without overlooking the need to be a place of pastoral care.

After many years without one, I now needed someone alongside me in a paid role, who was ordained and licensed as a minister. We did have a potential solution. Paul Wilkinson was on our team as an Ordained Local Minister (OLM) but he had a full-time job and his time availability was therefore limited. However, he was already looking to restructure his working pattern as a way of making two days a week available to the church. One day he came to see me, believing that God was saying it needed to be a full-time commitment. My response was, 'OK, let's see what God will do.'

Alongside this, I felt that we needed to model a greater synergy between how the lead minister was paid and how the rest of the staff team were paid. We were called to be a pioneering, missionary church and this needed to be reflected in the way in which we paid our lead minister. It needed to be more lightweight and flexible, enabling us to respond to changing needs and opportunities and to release others into paid positions as necessary. Especially within the historic denominations we need alternative models for how we pay church leaders and a more flexible approach to the way in which leaders are appointed, rethinking the relationship between lay and ordained and making space for leaders of churches to be raised up from within the community.

So I proposed that I transfer from stipendiary ministry to self-supporting ministry with the anticipation that the Fountain of Life would pay me at the level of an incumbent's stipend, but with me responsible for making my own housing and pension arrangements. The church would be 'losing' the minister's house provided by the diocese, but the gift two years earlier of a property meant that effectively the Fountain of Life had its own accommodation for a minister in the future if necessary.

We agreed this way forward with the Fountain of Life trustees and the bishop, and purchased the house from the diocese, which also enabled us to adapt our home to provide suitable accommodation for Pippa's mother. We renegotiated our 'parish share' with the diocese to remain a nett contributor to costs of diocesan mission, training and support, but with the Fountain of Life responsible for paying its own local costs direct to its ministers. At my own request, I received 80 per cent of a full stipend to release time for other activities outside the church. In my mind, all of this would enable us to step into appointing Paul at least part-time on a paid basis.

We also held a Gift Day and this amazingly enabled us to fund Paul full-time for at least a year. As usual, God's thoughts and plans were greater than ours and He enabled us, through the generosity of the Fountain family and Paul's willingness to step out in faith, to appoint him full-time as our associate minister from 1st February 2015, to take on pastoral and organisational responsibilities.

It didn't at this stage mean that Paul would be the person to eventually succeed me as leader, but this structure paved the way for transition. So let's now pick up the story again after our retreat in 2017, when God called us to pass on the baton of leadership. There were questions for us to address: What did the timescale look like? What did we need to put in place before we left? What were the steps in communicating well? What would we then be doing? What did our life look like if we took away 'leading the church'? What would the reaction of the church be? How could we prepare well to be a blessing for our successor? Were there things to stop?

The first step was to talk it over with our bishops and, as I had my regular Ministerial Development Review (MDR) coming up with our local suffragan bishop, Jonathan,[163] the Bishop of Lynn, this seemed to be the place to start. As we have always been a church with a ministry across the diocese, I had

---

[163] Rt Rev Jonathan Meyrick, Bishop of Lynn 2011–2021.

previously tended to meet up more often with the Bishop of Norwich, then Graham James, who was used to me contacting him from time to time to discuss possible initiatives, but Bishop Jonathan was also a very supportive and encouraging bishop. So this seemed to be the ideal opportunity to raise the issue of leadership change and the wisest strategic timetable. He listened and we explored the timing further, agreeing that the summer of 2019 would give us all time to prepare well. He also assured me that if it was the church's desire to appoint Paul as my successor then he would be supportive. This seemed further confirmation that the time was indeed right.

The life of the church seemed to be healthy. From that perspective also, it felt just the right time to be handing over. Financially the church was in good shape which, given the propensity for leadership change to be a bumpy ride, would give a buffer if there were difficulties. My associate, Paul, was growing in confidence and authority. He was well respected and his ministry welcomed and appreciated. He was ready for the next step of leading a church. Whether or not he would be appointed to lead this one was not ours to decide upon, but if the Fountain did want this to happen, then we wanted to do all we could to make it possible.

The next step was to speak to the leadership team. This was a bit more tricky because I wanted to tell the staff team first, followed by the trustees, and then make it public to the church as soon after that as possible. So in March 2018 I told the staff team and relied upon their discretion and confidentiality. The immediate response was disappointingly positive! There was a measure of sadness and some trepidation, but the response was summed up for me by our administrator, Karen, who said, 'I have never been in a church that has handled leadership transition so well.' Of course, the only problem was that it hadn't actually happened yet! But we were encouraged by her response, for she was commenting more on the process and the timetable rather than the actual outcome.

The staff were so good at keeping it to themselves. I wrote to all the trustees, met personally with the bishop's trustees[164] and then announced the plan to the church at the annual meeting. I would step down at the end of June 2019, just over a year hence, and my successor would be appointed to start as close to 1st July as possible. This gave the church, the bishops and not least Paul time to resolve the question of who would be the next leader of the Fountain of Life. It didn't take long. Three months later, by the end of July 2018, that question had been answered. The church was unanimous that Paul was the man, and the bishops were in agreement. I interview Paul about his story of vision and call in Appendix Four.

Now we could focus on the things that needed to be put in place and resolved before the transition happened. One of the areas that I wanted to strengthen during this year was that of the preaching and teaching team. Paul and I more or less alternated leading services and preached regularly. Our all-age worship services were mostly led by our gifted lay ministry team. As well as visiting speakers, there were individuals within the congregation who I invited to preach. Wendy, our much loved Lay Licensed Minister (formerly reader), who had been so faithful and constant in her service and regularly preached or led services, was now about to retire. So we needed to expand the team by appointing others to lead and preach in a way that would be formally recognised and approved by the diocese.

At the time, I was reminded of David selecting five stones in preparation for his battle with Goliath, in 1 Samuel 17. So I felt that we should be looking to appoint five people. The Church of England's Authorised Worship Assistants (AWA) scheme was a way of quickly obtaining the bishop's approval for those called to exercise a public ministry within the Church. It did not require the same measure of external selection and training as

---

[164] Bishop's trustees fulfil a similar function to a churchwarden within an Anglican church. A churchwarden is a lay person elected to serve as the bishop's representative in the parish, providing oversight of spiritual, legal, financial and practical aspects of church life.

the office of reader or LLM. Andrew and Julia, Dan, Karen and Tim were duly appointed by the trustees to exercise this ministry. They enjoyed the confidence of the congregation and it was seen as a very natural and positive step for them to take.

It is interesting to note that Jesus did not pass the baton of ushering in the kingdom to one person but to a team of at least eleven, and by the day of Pentecost this seems to have increased to 120 (Acts 1:15). Paul would be the one now to carry the baton as senior leader, but it was very good and heartening to be leaving a strong preaching team as well as a very gifted staff team.

So now we had resolved the timescale, found out who the new leader would be, communicated well and a new team had been assembled. What else could we do to prepare as well as possible? Were there things that needed to stop? Especially those that I was more directly involved in or had been involved in starting? What did I need to finish well so that Paul could start with as clean a sheet as possible? In the event, we identified three areas of our life together that needed to be resolved.

The *first of these activities* was the Fountain Network, which I had established to be a way of connecting with churches that valued our help and wanted to be in a purposeful relationship with us. It also provided a structure that would enable a missional community to remain in relationship with us if it grew into a self-governing Anglican church. However, since then, two things in particular had changed.

First, and most significant, was the change effected by the Fountain of Life being appointed as a resource church in the diocese. This not only enabled but actively encouraged churches to relate to us without the need for a separate network structure.

Second, New Wine's vision to network churches and leaders had been strengthened and reinvigorated under Paul Harcourt's leadership. Under this umbrella, Pippa and I already hosted a core group of leaders and as a church we were part of the New Wine family. With New Wine's renewed commitment to encouraging local partnership of churches and in particular to becoming a planting movement, it felt unnecessary to have another network alongside this one.

The Fountain Network wasn't a separate legal entity, as it existed under the authority of the Fountain of Life trustees, so it was an easy enough matter to simply bring it to a gentle conclusion. It had served its time, and its purpose would continue to be fulfilled by the church.

The *second area of activity* was our relationship with WTC. We always enjoyed an excellent relationship with WTC and its principal, Lucy Peppiatt. Lucy had been very supportive and appreciative of our positioning as a hub serving a rural area. However, with economies of scale to consider and the need for a hub to be viable in terms of student dynamics, there had been questions for some time as to whether we could continue to host the East Anglian hub in Ashill. In early 2019, it was agreed that it would move to Cambridge.

The *final area of activity* which we scheduled to finish was our leadership of the Boulder Gang programme for children aged ten to eleven at New Wine. Some of the core team from the Fountain of Life had indicated that they would be standing down after the fifth year of serving and this weakened our capacity to be the lead church for delivering the programme. So we gave New Wine the requisite notice and, while some of the team from Fountain of Life would continue to be part of the core team, the church would no longer be responsible for delivering the programme.

So, with the combination of these three 'closures', it felt to me as if we had laid to rest the things that needed to come to an end.

As has often been said, there is no success without succession. I have now been involved in two. First in 2005 when Martin passed the baton to me, and now here I was passing it on to Paul in 2019. I have experienced it both ways: receiving and giving. It occurred to me that there were things to learn from an athletics relay race.

At the point of handover, both runners have to be facing forward, looking ahead. Neither can afford to look back – neither the one giving nor the one receiving. In our context, Paul had to be looking ahead to the next stage of the race. Pippa and I should not look back, resting on what had been achieved, but needed to be looking forward to the next stage of our adventure in following Jesus and finishing the race well.

For it to be a smooth transition, at the point of handover both runners must be running at the same speed. Passing the baton on needs to happen when there is momentum and at the point when the next runner is ready to take it on. That was really important to me in the discernment process – Paul was ready to run.

Finally, at the point of handover it is the responsibility of the runner finishing to put the baton into the hand of the one who will take it on. It was my responsibility to finish well and give Paul the best possible start he could have. I'm sure there were things that Paul had to sort out, but I tried!

It is probably true that leadership succession from within is not always the right thing for a church. However, it is undoubtedly true that historically the Church of England has not practised succession from within often enough. It is sometimes argued that an interregnum (literally 'between the two reigns') is helpful for a church. It is said that it gives people emotional space to recover from the previous vicar's departure (or leadership!), the opportunity to consider the vision of the church and type of leader sought after (normally married with a young family is top of the list), and mobilises the people in the church to step up in the absence of a vicar. However, if a church is alive, is united around a vision and has a healthy, mobilised body of Christ already released into ministry, then it is continuity of vision and leadership that is needed rather than the brakes of an interregnum being imposed. The latter usually leads to losing people, finances, momentum and vision. In worst case scenarios, the new vicar comes in with not only a very different vision but also conflicting values, which can easily break a church rather than build it up. This is not imaginary. There are unfortunately many real cases where this has happened, often to the extreme detriment of building the kingdom; not to mention the emotional and relational cost to many faithful and committed people.

In my view, succession from within for the senior leadership of the church mitigates against this danger. However, it is healthy and wise – even essential – to be looking out for opportunities to bring others into leadership from outside the local church community at the supportive tier of leadership. This brings in the very necessary leadership resources, experience and wisdom from other places, guards against complacency and comfort, brings in the dynamic of change and gives space for new ideas and ways to be explored. But all within the parameters of the underlying vision and DNA of the church remaining unchanged.

There are many examples in the Bible of succession working well: Moses to Joshua (Deuteronomy 31:7-8; 34:9), David to Solomon (1 Kings 1:30), Paul to Timothy (1 Timothy 1:2) and Titus (Titus 1:4), as well as to many others in a church-planting context such as Priscilla and Aquila (Acts 18:19). At the time of our handover to Paul (not St Paul!), it was the story of Elijah passing on to Elisha that caught my eye (2 Kings 2). Elisha was one of a school of prophets, there are more miracles attributed to him in Scripture than to Elijah, and even after his death his bones had the capacity to bring life (2 Kings 13:21). I felt that under Paul's leadership this was a promise of growth in the miraculous, the prophetic and life in the Spirit. I pray it will be so.

Transition is not restricted to the way in which we have developed the senior leadership within this church. We have always encouraged leaders of a ministry to be looking for the person God is raising up behind them. Ministries continue in the church so long as we have champions for them. Tim, having pioneered and developed Kidz Klub, still had a vision to be involved at a strategic level but recognised the need to pass on the running of the local Kidz Klub to someone else. Having prayed, he recognised in Matt a young man with the gifting and call to take it on, so Tim began to draw alongside Matt, encourage and nurture him until it was time to release him into that role.

Similarly, Martin Spaul recognised in Adam a young man who had the potential to be his successor as youth worker, and over the course of a year, Martin intentionally gave him opportunities to grow and invested time and energy in his development. More recently, another young man, Joe, was appointed with the intention for him to succeed Maryanne in taking on her Kidz Klub responsibilities. This has now taken place. Our small-group leaders are encouraged to appoint assistants and to involve every member in the leadership of the group. All our other ministry team leaders are encouraged to be looking out for people in whom they can invest with a view to releasing them into their role.

Growth is often accelerated as we release the things we have grown comfortable in to others and step into new challenges for ourselves. Let's do all we can to pass on our experience of successes and failures in such a way as to enable others to go further than we would ever be able to go ourselves. A concept many leaders have referred to is that our ceiling should be the next generation's floor.[165] An excellent way of putting it.

A few years ago I heard Fanny Waterman interviewed on *Desert Island Discs*.[166] As a young married woman she was a pianist who performed at many concerts. She was concerned about all the travelling but her husband, Geoffrey, himself a doctor and music enthusiast, said to her something along the lines that he was there so she could fly. Eventually she had children and gave up the concert tour and concentrated on

---

[165] A term used by many but I believe originates from Eric Thomas, see www.amazon.com/1036-Eric-Thomas-Ceiling-Generations/dp/B08KYWM4PP (accessed 6th April 2021).

[166] www.bbc.co.uk/programmes/b00sw7fd (accessed 22nd January 2021).

teaching. In 1961 she founded the Leeds International Piano Competition and this kick-started the career of many professional musicians. Her motivation in doing this was so that 'others might fly'. Her husband's commitment to her in turn envisioned and enabled her to help others go further than she had.

It's a great picture of marriage and the call to submit to one another (Ephesians 5:21). In marriage, husbands and wives are called to commit themselves to the flourishing of the other. But it's also a great picture of the Church as family too. We are called to prefer one another (Romans 12:10, KJV), to honour one another, to rejoice over one another's successes and joys and to do all we can to see others flourish. Intentional transition of leadership at all levels is one way in which we can encourage this to happen.

As I have said, I have experience of this both ways. There are challenges about it, especially in our context of experiencing succession while maintaining the presence of both the incoming and outgoing leader. It requires a maturity and humility from both to enable it to work well. There are potential dangers or rocks upon which such succession can founder.

One potential rock is that of comparison. Paul addresses this in 1 Corinthians 12 while considering the gifts of the Spirit. Using the human body as a metaphor he addresses, on the one hand, issues of inferiority – for example, the foot saying, 'Because I am not a hand, I do not belong to the body' (v15) – and, on the other hand, issues of superiority – for example, the head saying to the feet, 'I don't need you!' (v21). It's hard to stop other people making comparisons, but biblical humility is neither cultivating a spirit of superiority nor is it about subservience. True humility is found in working alongside one another, recognising the unique contribution and value of each other in an equal way. Comparison often leads to a critical spirit. The incoming leader needs to exercise grace and wisdom in honouring the work that has preceded them, while not being afraid to change the way things are done and to set new vision.

We cannot afford to have any 'sacred cows'. The outgoing leader needs to let go.

A further rock that sometimes arises is that of competition. Saul did not handle well David growing in popularity with the people and being accredited with more victories in battle than him (1 Samuel 18:7-9). It is important for both leaders to measure outcomes objectively rather than comparatively. In our case, Martin laid the foundations, I built on these and Paul will, in the grace of God, develop the 'house of God' even further than either of us. It is all part of seeing the kingdom come. We need to be settled about the value of our contribution. If it becomes an issue for us, then it would suggest that our identity is rooted in performance as a servant rather than in our position as a son or daughter.

Another potential rock is what I would call 'collusion'. At an early stage in the story of David and his son Absalom, the latter is described as acting in a way that 'stole the hearts of the people of Israel' (2 Samuel 15:6). This is something for the previous leader to watch in their own heart. Leaders forge deep relationships with members of their church. It would be unnatural for the outgoing leader to stop pastorally caring for those they have been in relationship with, but we all know when a line has been crossed that undermines the new leader's position. This is not an easy one to define. It is perhaps a matter of integrity. We need to be aware of the fickleness of the human heart and make sure that our motives in connecting with people are pure. The development of factions within the church happens all too easily and was another problem Paul had to address in Corinth (1 Corinthians 1:12).

There are three ways of helping to ensure succession works well. First, it can help for there to be clear boundaries agreed between the incoming and outgoing leader, which need to be respected. On each occasion here, the outgoing leader has initially taken six months leave of absence from the church. This prevents the status quo being prolonged in an unhealthy manner. Everyone must get used to looking towards the new leader for direction, guidance and leadership. Actually, as the outgoing leader, I was very happy about this as it enabled me to take a sabbatical gap which we mostly spent doing all the things we hadn't had the time to do since getting married in 1984! Six months may seem a long time, but it soon passes, and is necessary to create the clean break.

In both our transitions the outgoing leader has at least initially continued to be part of the church. In our context, I have felt it to be a more appropriate model for the outgoing leader not to return to holding a formal position within the church structure. Their supportive presence to the new leader is potentially a tremendous strength in the new season, and their ongoing relationship with others in the church community can also be an important contributor in ensuring stability and confidence. But it is a new season and it's important that the new leader not only grows in their own identity and style, but also develops the team around them. The existing team members may need space and time to transition their hearts as well as minds to accepting the new leader.

Second, there is the importance of establishing good communication channels. These patterns will no doubt evolve and change over the years. Having for so long been at the centre of decision-making and at the heart of the team, the outgoing leader has to get used to no longer feeling the pulse of the church. They won't know the details and be as up to speed on new developments as they once were. There will be times when they will, like everyone else, hear of important developments through communications from the church rather than in a pre-informed way. It feels strange for a while! On the other hand, the incoming leader needs to define their own leadership and not be seen to be deferring to the previous leader, even though it may be wise to consult them from time to time. As in all other relationships, it helps to stay in regular, open communication with each other, recognising any issues that have arisen and resolving niggles before they escalate into more serious relationship problems. It helps to keep on defining the relationship.

Finally, it's important to keep remembering and accepting who's leading. It's the incoming leader now who should be calling the shots, taking decisions. The outgoing leader needs to respect the changes and not expect to be asked or consulted.

In all these three areas, the onus, I think, is on the outgoing leader. They need to exercise grace and wisdom, not least in speaking well of their successor, never making public or private criticism, and giving as much personal encouragement and support to their successor as is possible. I would hope to fulfil that as well as my predecessor, Martin Down, modelled it for me.

Final Word

So, there it is. The story of how God has worked here. It's not intended to be read as a 'how to' book. It's a story specific to us. You may well share our vision to see the Church renewed and society transformed, but the details of what that looks like will be specific to your context. I hope, though, that in our narrative there are some shared stories and principles that have resonated with you. Hopefully you will have been encouraged and challenged to see the kingdom come more in your own life and in your church and community.

It is healthy for us to allow others to speak into our lives and the churches we lead. For the past ten years, Pippa and I have been so blessed to enjoy the friendship, love and support of our closest mentors, Bob and Mary Hopkins. As well as leading ACPI, Bob and Mary have served on the Fresh Expressions team since its formation and been involved in many of the movements of multiplying church over the past forty-five years. They have accompanied us on our journey too. I asked them a couple of years ago to give me their assessment of the hallmarks of the Fountain of Life. It sparked a conversation out of which I have drawn the following ten cultures which have been helpful to keep in mind when watching over our life together.

Culture of the Spirit

Our life together has been marked by a wholehearted embrace of an immanent Godhead with an openness to the Spirit. Consistently in our life together we have sought to make space for the Holy Spirit to move upon us and lead us into His purposes and plans. In the end, lives have been transformed, not through natural wisdom or by clever strategies, but by ordinary people encountering the extraordinary God of the Bible. The Holy Spirit is the best person able to fill us with God's love and empower us to live as disciples of Jesus. This foundational value infuses our life together and informs all that we do, and I cannot overstate its significance. It is the Holy Spirit who is the Lord and giver of life.

Culture of the Word

There is no renewal without the renewal of the ministry of God's Word. Inviting God to anoint our preaching and teaching so as to bring life-giving change to the hearers through the words we speak. Preaching the good news, the full gospel of salvation and wholeness in a way that invites application to our day-to-day lives and encourages people to make a response. A culture that is formed by choosing to sit under the authority of the Word in a way that shapes our lives and our interaction with the culture of the world. The Word is intended to bring transformation, not just impart information.

Culture of hospitality and welcome

A real commitment to building church as family that has an integrity and authenticity. A place of extraordinary welcome and hospitality, where we work hard to be genuinely known and loved as we care for one another and accept one another, as Christ accepts us.

Culture of empowerment

Equipping and releasing every member of the body of Christ to excel in their gifts and ministries and see the kingdom come. It's a culture that produces leaders in the kingdom. This leads to multiplication as each person is supported to grow and develop into their call and vision. We can be very good at teaching and training, but never give people the opportunity to develop and grow through experience. Alternatively, we can release people but fail to give the tools and support that enable them to fly. Growing people into maturity requires us to do both.

Culture of sacrificial giving

An understanding that following Jesus has a cost and a commitment attached. This has been reflected in extraordinary outpourings of financial generosity. Yet it is a generosity of a lifestyle that is beyond the giving of money. It is also reflected in the amount of time given, care shown in practical ways, a willingness to share life together and to prefer the needs of others to our own.

Culture of 'both–and'

We have looked for ways of embracing the tension created by equal and opposite ideas, rather than feeling forced to choose between them – 'both–and' rather than 'either–or'. We think 'big' and act 'small'. We are both 'gathered' at the hub and 'scattered', especially in missional communities. We are both 'large' and 'attractional' when we gather together, but 'small', 'emerging' and 'engaged' in our missional communities. We invite people to 'come' and we commission them to 'go'.

Culture of vision and team

As much as possible, everything that we do as a church is led by someone with a vision and passion for that aspect of our life together. These 'champions' are then encouraged to gather teams around them who share their vision and passion and to look for those who will be their successors. This develops sustainable, long-term fruitfulness.

Culture of perseverance

For most of the past twenty-five years we have been at the cutting edge of change within the Church of England, pioneering a new form of church. We have been provocative, and at times there have been disappointments, struggles, misunderstandings, hurts and hardships. We have been described as 'loyal radicals': committed to mission and new ways of being church, but equally committed to doing so within the framework of the Church of England. It has required us to exercise faith and patience and to practise resilience. In all the changing circumstances and challenges, our unifying core vision has been to see His kingdom come.

Culture of incarnation

We have sought to prioritise the forming of church around how Jesus is working in a particular community, rather than imposing a preconceived idea or model of church. Allowing mission to shape the church rather than vice versa. Looking to see where God is already at work as we listen to the community and to the Father. This places an emphasis on relationship rather than rule; on activity as a response to community needs and listening to God, rather than pre-formed plans; on openness to new ways of engagement and an authority structure which is 'low on control … high on accountability'.[167]

Culture of mission

Church and mission are indivisible terms. You can't have one without the other. A church in mission mode is more than adding a few bolt-on extras. It's a culture shift. A culture of mission is one in which the whole church is facing outwards. The mission imperative forged the birthing of the Fountain of Life and has since shaped our development and growth. Rather like the explorers of the Wild West, we have pioneered, built a settlement and then pioneered again. Again, like the experience of the apostle Paul, we can say that 'Christ's love compels us' to fulfil the commission Jesus Himself gave us: 'Go and make disciples of all nations, baptising them in the name of the Father

---

[167] Hopkins and Breen, *Clusters: Creative Mid-Sized Missional Communities*, pp 39,141; see www.3dmovements.com (accessed 1st February 2021).

and of the Son and of the Holy Spirit, and teaching them to obey everything I have commanded you. And surely I am with you always, to the very end of the age' (2 Corinthians 5:14; Matthew 28:19-20). That has been our experience as we have engaged in 'redigging the wells' here in deepest rural Norfolk, and it will also be yours as you go in His name.

I finish the final edit of this book in March 2021 on the centenary of the last revival in England, which began in Lowestoft in March 1921, before spreading throughout East Anglia during the following summer and later in the year to Scotland and Ulster too. It began the year after this nation's last great pandemic of Spanish flu.

> *Will you not revive us again,*
> *that your people may rejoice in you?*
> *(Psalm 85:6)*

Finally let me tell you what you already know:

God is good.[168]

He is faithful.[169]

He equips those He calls.[170]

He promises to live in us.[171]

He looks for obedience not perfection.[172]

---

[168] Psalm 100:5.
[169] 1 Corinthians 1:9.
[170] Exodus 4:10-12.
[171] Galatians 2:20.
[172] 2 John 1:6.

He will build His Church.[173]

His kingdom will endure forever.[174]

Maranatha! Come, Lord Jesus.[175]

[173] Matthew 16:18.
[174] Luke 1:33.
[175] 1 Corinthians 16:22.

He will build His Church...

His Kingdom will endure forever...

Who is this Christ, Lord Jesus?

Appendix One
Legal Structure of the Fountain of Life

In terms of our legal charitable status, we were initially established as an Unincorporated Charitable Association.[176] This afforded us legal standing outside the Church of England. However, the governance of the charitable trust was then established in a similar way to a parish church.

Trustees were elected in a similar way to a Parochial Church Council (PCC) by members of the church at the Annual General Meeting (AGM),[177] with each trustee appointed to serve for a maximum of four years. There was a maximum of twelve trustees appointed in this way. At our very first AGM these were appointed to serve for staggered terms so that each year hence there would usually be three vacancies to be filled. Trustees who have served their term are not allowed to stand again until at least two years have lapsed. This provides continuity but also ensures fresh faces and voices can be seen and heard.

Trustees also include a Deanery Synod[178] representative (elected at the AGM to serve for three years) as is common with

---

[176] Later, in 2014, we changed this to a Charitable Incorporated Organisation when this option was introduced by the Charity Commission, as it was more appropriate for our size.

[177] This functioned in a similar way to the Annual Parochial Church Meeting held by a parish church.

[178] The Church of England adopts a synodical form of governance and the Deanery Synod is the local form of this. Each Deanery Synod consists of clergy and elected lay members of the churches within that deanery.

other Anglican churches. Ordained or licensed lay leaders serve as ex officio members. There can also be up to four non-voting co-opted trustees, which gives some flexibility if there are particular areas of our life together on which we need to focus.

Each year the trustees appoint two of their number to serve as bishop's trustees, which is our way of describing the office of churchwarden. They do not have very much gold or silver to look after, but they do create a clear accountability structure and line of access to the bishops for the congregation separate to the vicar and staff.

Appendix Two
Covenant Between Ministers of the Parish Churches and Fountain of Life[179]

This is a Covenant of grace rather than law. It is a sign of our agreement to seek to work together in partnership for the sake of the world and the gospel. We recognise and value each other's call to build up the community of God's people and present the gospel afresh to this generation.

We believe that our intention to seek unity in the midst of our diversity will result in God's blessing upon our churches and communities and will increase our fruitfulness in ministry and mission.

Joint Values of Ministry

1. We value and welcome our unity in the one God: Father, Son and Holy Spirit.

2. We value and welcome each other's diversity in forms of worship and church life as part of our strength in mission. We rejoice in variety, believing that it reflects the infinite creativity of God.

3. We value each other's journey of faith, recognising the way that God has sovereignly called us to engage in His mission to the world.

---

[179] Edited for the purpose of this book.

4. We value our mutual partnership of parochial and network church ministry.

5. We value the ministry of reconciliation entrusted to us by our Lord Jesus Christ and commit ourselves afresh to living together in that same spirit of reconciliation.

6. We value and affirm our joint calling as the people of God to be a blessing to the local community.

Joint Expressions of our covenant relationship

1. We shall seek to live in love, unity and peace with one another. We seek to respond to God's love and creativity by working towards greater cooperation and reconciliation.

2. We shall pray for one another's ministry and witness.

3. We shall seek ways of cooperating together in common witness and service to the local community.

4. We shall look for ways in which we can share resources, gifts or skills with one another while recognising the priority of our respective callings.

5. We shall meet together regularly, not less than three times a year, for mutual encouragement, support, prayer, sharing of plans and activities. In this way, we shall increase our understanding of each other.

The Fountain of Life, as a network church, draws people from a wide geographical area and, therefore, the Fountain of Life may well be engaged in activities that require it to engage in consultation with clergy and church leaders in parishes beyond those embraced in this Covenant. This Covenant will inform these relationships.

Appendix Three
Internship Testimonies

Here are some comments from those who have successfully completed our internship programme:

> The internship at Fountain of Life [FoL] gave me so many opportunities to explore my gifting and the things I love doing. I discovered joy in working with children and musical worship, and the teaching from many wise people ignited a passion in me to learn. So here I am at theology college! My confidence and relationship with God grew and grew, and I am so thankful to FoL for that.
> *Rosie*

> The internship gave me a new start and established rules for my life. There were some great leaders around that were inspiring and mentoring us in different ways. I was very blessed and excited to be able to offer creativity to the Fountain and this was what I felt was my main contribution during my internship year. For me, this was a hugely defining time.
> *Adam*

> I enrolled in the Fountain of Life internship programme when I was eighteen, just after I left school. The greatest impact for me was being able to take part in the incredible work the church was doing. There was so much going on all the time, which meant there were always things to learn and people to learn from. I was constantly blown

away by the passion and gifting of the ministry leaders, and the impact they were having in rural Norfolk. The internship helped me grow closer to God, discover my calling and gave me the skills and gifts to carry out that calling in the future.

Matt

My year as an intern was definitely a year of growth. Through mentorship as well as through living with people in the congregation I learned so much of what made me who I am today. I really felt part of the family and it gave me an understanding of the phrase 'it takes a village to raise a child'.[180] I got to try so many things, fail at some, and discover sides of myself as a worship leader I only would've known through working closely with people who had gone before me. The love and support I had around me was nothing like I'd had before and something that's shaped me immensely, and that I'm forever grateful for.

Clara

My year gave me insight, training, a chance to explore my gifting and test my calling, but most importantly it gave me time and experience to allow God to open my eyes to what could be possible, and a hunger to join Him in whichever direction He took me.

Matt

---

[180] African proverb.

Appendix Four
Interview with Paul Wilkinson

How did you come to join the Fountain of Life?

My wife, Colette, and I arrived in Ashill in August 1996 with our eldest daughter, Rebecca, who was just eight weeks old. We came six weeks after The New Thing had been formed. I quickly found work as head gardener on a private estate and we settled in. We knew the church quite well before we moved to Ashill because it had been Colette's home for several years before she met and married me. We were excited at the prospect of being involved in a church that was moving in the power of the Holy Spirit, although that in itself was a new thing for me. I'd given my life to Christ in 1985 and had been fairly static in my faith until we moved here.

I remember, that autumn, having the most profound encounter with Jesus during a prayer ministry time in Ashill Community Centre. It felt as if I was given the opportunity to see Jesus on the cross and to witness His sacrifice first-hand. There was a moment when He turned His head towards me as I stood in the crowd on the hill at Golgotha, and He looked directly at me. It was the moment I can truly say that I understood that His death and subsequent resurrection were a personal gift for me, for each of us, and that He sees us all as His dearest and most precious friends. That was the day I was filled with the Holy Spirit and it was also the moment that I began to sense His calling on my life.

How did your calling to leadership emerge?

Being 'called' is a strange experience because I found myself testing, checking and seeking confirmation that it really was a call from God over and over until I had a sense that He was saying, 'Come on, Paul, how much more do you need to hear before you do something?!' So, hesitantly, I spoke to Martin Down, our vicar at the time, and the process of selection for ordained ministry began. At that time, after a period of about two and a half years, I was told that I wasn't quite what they were looking for. I came away from the experience wondering what it had all been about, and feeling more than a little angry at God and the church that after all the form-filling, interviews and exercises it was a 'no'.

Life, however, moved on. Our second daughter, Kezia, arrived in 1999 and my career in Quality Assurance, Environmental and Health and Safety Management (QEHS) developed quite rapidly. At the Fountain, I'd learned to lead worship with the band, undertaken a preaching course Martin put on, ran a home group and a pastorate, but the sense of calling to ordination never left me. I remember one Sunday morning after I'd preached a sermon, God said quite clearly, 'Now.' It wasn't an audible voice – it was as if my whole being resonated with the word – and there was nothing else other than that one word.

By now Martin had stepped down as leader of the Fountain of Life and Stephen was the senior minister, so I spoke to him and the selection process started again. This time I applied to become an Ordained Local Minister (OLM), which is non-stipendiary and would be based at the Fountain of Life, a church I assumed I would never lead in my own right. This time the answer was 'yes' and, to cut a long story very short, I was ordained as priest in 2011, by which time I'd risen to the lofty heights of UK and Ireland manager for QEHS and had worked all over the country and occasionally in Europe.

Looking back now, I can see that during my initial application for ordination, God showed me where He was going to take me, but He knew I wasn't ready for it then, so He put me in a place where I could learn and be equipped. He loves to provide well for His children!

How did you feel when you were appointed to succeed Stephen?

The truly amazing thing for me in this journey has been that I've seen the church grow, from the time when it was a tender but vibrant cutting taken from the root stock of the parish church with Martin tending it, to the strong and vigorous plant that it has become in the years it's been led by Stephen. So I'm truly humbled to have been given the role of senior minister now. It is such a privilege and I pray that God guides me and the rest of our great team to sow new seeds in the right places.

How has Covid-19 impacted the life of the church?

I'm not sure we'll understand the full impact of Covid-19 until it's gone, but there have been some significant effects. Initially we didn't think it would last long, so we set about running church online, prerecording our services, with a view to maintaining a sense of family and connection. Our team learned new skills rapidly and managed to create a vibrant, high-quality online presence for all ages. Realising it wasn't going to end quickly, we installed cameras and new equipment so that we could livestream the services to add a sense of immediacy to our worship. At Christmas and New Year, we managed to engage with the church family during the service, sharing greetings and words of knowledge.[181] I can now see that post-pandemic, our online presence must continue to meet the needs of those who can't or don't often come.

Some of the pastoral structures we had in place struggled to engage electronically while others flourished. In some areas we had to work much harder at addressing needs, and I think the

---

[181] 1 Corinthians 12:8.

impact of that will continue for some time to come. Remarkably, some words of knowledge and pictures we received six months before the pandemic spoke into the situation we found ourselves in. These encouraged us to be particularly attentive to the way in which we as a church family cared for one another. Periodically, I encouraged each one of us to be looking out for three to five people, making contact and providing a listening ear or practical support as necessary. In this way we would minimise the number who slipped through the net.

There was a time between lockdowns when we opened our doors again and welcomed as many in as our risk assessment would permit. Within a few weeks we were almost at capacity and wondering how to cope with the restrictions and a growing group of returnees. Should we open a second venue or start a second service? How could we incorporate face-to-face kids' church and youth work with limited numbers and extended spacing? Then the second lockdown happened, followed by a third. But all that points towards a future filled with possibilities. No doubt some may not return, but equally there will be some new faces who will cross the threshold.

What are your hopes for the future?

The Fountain of Life feels to me as if it has established its roots now. It's matured to the point where it is entering its most productive stage of life. It's bursting to grow more and to reach the places that haven't yet seen the glory of God's goodness. My belief is that Jesus wants all the people, in this and every other corner of the earth, to know that He gave His life for us and that there is hope and life to be found in Him. I pray the seeds we sow from here on will become mighty oaks that glorify His name and His kingdom.